WORRIPITHICUS ANXIETUS

The Joy of Worry

The Joy of Worry

by Ellis Weiner

Illustrations by Roz Chast

CHRONICLE BOOKS

SAN FRANCISCO

Library of Congress Cataloging-in-Publication Data available.

ISBN 0-8118- 4139-1

Manufactured in Canada.

Designed by Kyle Blue Inc., San Francisco, CA.

Distributed in Canada by Raincoast Books
9050 Shaughnessy Street
Vancouver, British Columbia V6P 6E5

10 9 8 7 6 5 4 3 2 1

Chronicle Books LLC
85 Second Street
San Francisco, California 94105
www.chroniclebooks.com

To my mother, who taught me to worry about everything, and to my father, who taught me not to worry.

— E. W.

CONTENTS

INTRODUCTION

Worry and Be Happy

"Worry," Benjamin Franklin wrote, "is like a rocking chair. It will give you something to do, but it won't get you anywhere."
So said one of America's first Wise Men. Franklin, who of course was right about everything, in this instance was wrong.

After two and a half centuries of scientific, medical, and technological progress, we now know that worry is not, as Franklin thought, a fruitless but an absorbing form of pre-occupation. Nor is it merely a symptom of "poor humour" or "melancholia" or "morbid negativity." *Worry is in fact an exciting, dynamic mental state that, when mastered, can be used to attain happiness, success, romance, and fun!*

In the pages that follow you will learn how to approach the subject of worry, free of the old preconceptions; you will learn how to celebrate worry and how to use worrying to obtain what you want.

Worry: What It Is

Worry is fear harnessed to imagination.

Shortly after we perceive something (an event, a person, a thought, etc.), our brain starts to consider the possible outcomes, repercussions, or implications of the something. And, because our brains are powerful and efficient, the list of negative or bad things that can happen grows at a fantastic rate. We become apprehensive and scared, and we experience these sensations as worry. Although we often attempt to ignore or deny these feelings, sooner or later the fears assert themselves and we have to admit it: we're worried.

It is important to understand that a worrying person is uneasy or nervous or scared or terrified not of what is actually happening but of *what might happen.* That is the brilliance, the beauty, the power, the triumph of worry. Because *anything* might happen. The potential of worry is infinite.

Taxonomy of Worry

Worry is not a single, monolithic thing, an undifferentiated fear of bad things to come. There are many gradations of worry, from the mild to the severe, each with its own emotional and physical manifestations.

The chart on page 14 shows a basic continuum of worry, although many other possible forms of worrying fall within or even beyond this range. "Chafing," for example, might be placed between "Fretting" and "Brooding," while "Freaking out" might be placed after "Panicking." But these five are enough for our purposes, and we will refer to them in the pages that follow.

Basic Worry Types

Type of Worry	Emotional Characteristics	Physical Manifestations	Evasive Verbal Response (to "What's wrong?")
"JUST THINKING"	Normal affect; intellectual distraction with slight emotional disquiet.	Distant look; slight, nonalarming stillness.	"What? Oh, nothing. Just thinking."
FRETTING	Sourness; dawning unhappiness; mild alarm.	Outright frown; occasional nervous tic or pacing.	"I guess . . . oh, never mind. It's nothing."
BROODING	Extreme passivity; depressed affect. Emotional sluggishness; deep preoccupation.	Staring; sitting very still; alarming unresponsiveness.	"Nothing."
STEWING	Simmering mental agitation at a low boil becoming increasingly heated.	Fidgeting; barely contained restlessness.	"I don't want to talk about it."
PANICKING	Terror; shutdown of normal rational and emotional function; obliviousness to external input.	Wild-eyed gesturing, extreme agitation. Shortness of breath and accelerated heart rate.	"What do you mean, 'What's wrong?'!"

The Way of the Worrier

The path of the successful worrier begins with an understanding of the origins of worry, leading then from a recognition of the subtle differences between the many states of worrying to an acceptance—indeed, an embrace—of worry.

To harness this powerful force, the student of worrying must learn to worry deliberately, consciously, and in a targeted and directed manner. Free-floating anxiety, spontaneous hand-wringing, general and uncontrolled not-knowing-what-to-do—these are for the unenlightened.

Through controlled worrying you will be able to lose weight, become healthier, advance your career, improve your love life, become both a better parent and a better driver, and achieve many more of your goals. Well-being, satisfaction, power, influence, *and joy* can be yours when you become a skilled worrier.

This book shows you how.

WEIGHT AND DIET

Worry Your Weight Away!

Isn't there any way to lose weight that doesn't involve starvation diets or surgery?

There is. You can actually lose weight—where you want, when you want—*by worrying.*

Everyone knows that persons under great stress, subjected to bouts of intense anxiety, drop pounds and slim down, appearing drawn and wasted in ways that the rest of us can only envy. Wouldn't it be great to be able to harness that emaciating power at will, for when you really need it—a summer at the beach, an important date or public appearance, a big job interview, or just any old time you want to feel trim and attractive?

You can, and it couldn't be easier.

You see, fat is imprisoned in our bodies in little "jails" called *fat cells.* Worrying puts stress on every system of the body; the musculature tenses, the nerves fray, the organs grind, the heart murmurs, and the mind reels. This causes the body to burn *calories,* or units of heat. As the calories burn, the fat cells "catch fire" and, in the ensuing confusion, the "inmates" "escape." The imprisoned bits of fat "bust out of jail" and "run away." They are thus free to be flushed from the body by normal excretory processes, and you lose weight.

But if worrying causes you to burn fat, why do people on diets remain overweight? After all, people on diets do nothing *but* worry. They worry about their weight, and their diets, and their clothes, and their cholesterol levels, and whether it's really true that food no one sees you eat doesn't make you gain weight. In fact, why aren't fat people the skinniest people around?

The reason is simple: *You cannot lose weight by worrying about losing weight.*

Paradoxical as it may sound, worrying about losing weight is not sufficiently stressful to cause weight loss. Overweight bodies build up a tolerance for weight-related worry, which means they don't burn significant numbers of calories while engaged in this type of worry.

To lose weight, then, it's necessary to worry about something *other* than losing weight. And that leaves a lot of possible topics— the universe is full of things to worry about.

Overweight, Overwrought, Overjoyed: The Three Types of Worry

There are three basic kinds of worrying that are effective for losing weight.

I. Global Worry

This common type of worrying is directed at topics that apply to everyone, everywhere—the environment, politics, the economy, epidemics, world crises, and so on. The good news is that they're easily found on TV, on the front pages of newspapers, on the radio, and in many other media outlets. But make sure your subject isn't too general. To think that you can grow thinner by worrying about

---

 For the tables in this section, Calories Burned totals are given per minute of worrying at Moderate Brooding. Actual results will vary depending on the subject's body type, medical and pharmaceutical history, and other factors.

Global Worry (Calories Burned)

Asteroid colliding with earth

Obliterates all life (312)

Obliterates some life but not politicians (722)

Awakens, enrages Godzilla (4)

Awakens, enrages Lenin (122)

Awakens, enrages J. Edgar Hoover (301)

Awakens, enrages Mongol hordes (1,690)

Awakens, enrages Liberace (13,870)

Global warming

Destruction of ozone layer (311)

Melting of polar ice caps (67)

Rising seas, beachfront housing destroyed (3,409)

Desertification of arable land (112)

Disrupted ecosystems (231)

Ski resorts absolutely ruined (5,890)

Airline industry suffers

Increased plane-change intervals at hubs (399)

Tighter restrictions on bargain fares (165)

Longer lines, fewer agents at counters (290)

Lengthy delays at security checkpoints (533)

Even less legroom between seats (312)

Even narrower seats (899)

Louder babies in adjacent rows (900)

Louder, abusive parents adjacent to babies (1,899)

More "snacks" served onboard (5,097)

Second Coming, Armageddon, exile of damned to Hell, 1,000-year reign of God on earth

Doesn't happen (12)

Happens (34,611)

Economic collapse

World banking system fails (290)

Automated Teller Machines (ATMs) run out of cash (2,311)

Chickens and eggs become new global currency (5,601)

Wallet, purse industry thrown into turmoil (6,099)

the economy is ridiculous. Such a large, all-embracing topic is too vague to ignite enough worry to burn significant calories. You must worry about various *aspects* of the economy, such as Sales of Existing Homes, the Balance of Trade, or the Manufacture of Durable Goods. (See table, "Global Worry," page 19.)

Even when focused in this way, Global Worry is general and, hence, more diffuse, making it less effective on your body—which is, after all, a relatively small part of the global picture. You'll experience some overall weight reduction, but you will be unable to target specific parts of your body. In fact, the larger and more ominous the subject, the fewer calories you actually burn. For example, the idea of global warming melting the glaciers, raising sea level by three inches all over the world, and inundating coastal cities is certainly disquieting—but how much, really, can you worry about it? If it happens, it happens.

2. Chain Worry

This kind of worrying is more advanced and challenging than global worrying. It demands higher levels of concentration, a more determined effort, and a broader knowledge of the issues of the world and of all the things there are to worry about. Because global worries are episodic, in that each subject is self-contained, they are limited in their duration and weight-reduction effects. In chain worrying however, as in a thermonuclear reaction, one thing leads to another. (See table, "Chain Worrying," facing page.)

Chain Worry permits you to take advantage of the Cumulative Effect of Mounting Panic (CEMP). Once you grasp the fact that one bad thing can lead to a worse thing, worrying gains momentum and can generate significant calories burned and weight lost.

However, while chain worrying may allow you to lose a lot of weight quickly by stewing yourself into a state of hysteria, you still won't be able to target specific body parts, such as hips or tummy. That requires an even more focused approach.

Chain Worrying (Calories Burned)

Major airline fails

Auto traffic increases (190)

Air pollution worsens (855)

Respiratory illnesses increase (132)

Admissions to hospitals increase (254)

Additional strain placed on already overworked nursing staff (365)

Stressed-out nurses become insubordinate to doctors (213)

Doctors become angry at nurse insubordination (304)

Doctors, distracted by anger, commit errors in medical practice (688)

Patients victimized by errors sue doctors (800)

Doctors successfully sued lose malpractice insurance,
cannot practice, and go bankrupt (122)

Bankrupt doctors resign from
country clubs (20)

Decline in dues-paying members
forces country clubs out of
business (101)

Failing country clubs shrink golf
industry (254)

Declining number of golfers leads to
decline in sales of golf shirts (30)

Golf shirt factories, based in
Southeast Asia, lay off workers (21)

Unemployed Southeast Asian textile
workers take to streets to protest (12)

Clash between workers and Southeast
Asian governments leads to open
conflict, civil unrest, military action,
quasi-military death squads, and
social and political chaos (4)

Total 4,365

Shortage of doctors strains health
care system (533)

Hospitals seek money-saving
measures (155)

Hospital kitchens ordered to cut
back on frills (265)

Desserts eliminated from
hospital menus (410)

National chocolate pudding
industry collapses (4,766)

Total 10,053

3. "It's All About Me" Worry

This is worrying at its finest, not just up close and personal but up close and self-obsessed. It's focused entirely on the individual's own personal concerns—work, friends, fun, spouse, lovers, children, and relatives. Instead of anguishing over the decimation of the rain forests, you'll worry about whether it will ruin your trip to Costa Rica next year. Where the global worrier would fret about the environmental impact of SUVs, you'll get anxious over whether the dealer will have the model and color you want in stock.

There's good news and bad news connected with this kind of worrying. The bad news is that these vexations, because they are so personal, can actually be unpleasant to experience. They're no longer just theoretical musings such as "Wouldn't it be awful if there were a swine flu epidemic?" Now it's more like "Maybe I should have used a condom last week after all."

However, the good news is that this kind of worry allows you to target specific parts of your body for slimming and trimming! Want more prominent check bones? Worry about your shrinking retirement portfolio. Dying to take inches off your waist? Brood about your four-year-old getting into Harvard. (See table, "'It's All About Me' Worrying," facing page and page 24.)

How is this possible? Frankly, medical science can't explain it yet. It's like acupuncture or reflexology: Western experts cannot say why sticking a pin in your forehead invigorates the spleen, or pressing your left big toe cures chicken pox. They just know that it does.

Similarly, worryologists are thus far baffled as to the variability of the results of worrying. For example, anxiety about your boyfriend's attractive new colleague typically—but not always—makes your ankles thinner.

---

 * CAUTION: Because results from "It's All About Me" Worrying are so significant and site-specific, use only Moderate Brooding or less (e.g., Fretting, "Just Thinking"). Anything stronger brings risk of severe muscles stiffness, organ collapse, or system failure.

For this reason, don't be afraid to deviate from the general guidelines in the table that follows. Experiment. Take notes. See what works. After all, it's your body. They're your worries. And only you can truly appreciate how wonderfully devastating and slimming they can be. Enjoy!

"It's All About Me" Worrying

Body Site or Part to Be Slimmed	Personal Worry Topic	Calories Burned
FACE	**Money**	
Cheeks	What if my retirement account shrinks to a tenth its current size?	455
Chin	What if I don't have a retirement account?	231
Lips	What if I will never be able to retire?	12
TORSO	**Children**	
Hips	What if my kid doesn't get into a good university?	944
Abdomen	What if my kid gets into a good university and never graduates?	2,890
Buttocks	What if my kid says she wants to go to law school?	103
Waist	What if my kid who says she wants to go to law school is four years old?	10,875
Left Shoulder	What if my kid has a crush on his teacher?	590
Right Shoulder	What if my kid, who has a crush on his teacher, is being home-schooled?	12,155
NECK, JOWLS	**Clothes**	
	What if my whole wardrobe is ugly?	366
	What if I have bad taste and don't know it?	460
	What if I can't afford decent clothes?	321
	What if I can't afford any clothes?	1,402
	What if I can't fit into my one good outfit?	204
	What if I did fit into my one good outfit, but now I can't get out of it?	6,822

"It's All About Me" Worrying *(continued)*

Body Site or Part to Be Slimmed	Personal Worry Topic	Calories Burned
HIPS	**Pets**	
	What if my dog is neurotic?	233
	What if I hate my cat?	122
	What if my cat hates me?	6,100
	What if I can't teach my bird to talk?	763
	What if my tropical fish die?	531
	What if my tropical fish lapse into a protracted coma?	410
	What if my hamster is sullen?	9
	What if my turtle "runs" away?	311
UPPER ARMS	**Relationships**	
	What if my partner and I don't talk?	732
	What if my partner and I don't do anything but talk?	8,102
	What if my partner and I hate each other's friends?	133
	What if my partner and I like each other's friends but hate each other?	890
ANKLES, FEET	**Spouse**	
	What if my spouse suddenly seems unhappy?	312
	What if my spouse suddenly seems a little too happy?	422
	What if my spouse has begun wearing a whole new wardrobe?	1,657
	What if my spouse has begun wearing my wardrobe?	5,096
	What if my spouse and I can't agree on whether or not to have children?	488
	What if my spouse and I can't agree on whether or not we have children?	12,098

Thin and Worried for Life: Keeping It Off

Some people believe that when they reach their target weight their lives will change fundamentally. They think they will feel so good about themselves that their careers will thrive, their love lives will blossom, and they'll be happy forever.

And there's the trap!

If you're happy, you'll stop worrying. And without worrying, how will you stay thin?

The solution, of course, is to keep worrying, no matter how good things threaten to become. *There's always something to worry about; you just need to find it.* There will always be poverty, starvation, enslavement, exploitation, strife, brutality, oppression, bad hair days, obnoxious relatives, and the risk that your worst personal secrets will (somehow) be revealed—to your family, to your employer, and to law enforcement personnel.

These are all subjects worthy of our deepest, most sincere worry. And for that we can only be thankful.

HEALTH AND FITNESS

Worrycising® Workouts for Wellness

"As long as you have your health, you have everything."

No one should actually believe this. Having your health doesn't mean you "have everything." It means you're in adequate shape to go out and get everything—but also, alas, to go out and *catch* everything. And, as every doctor knows, it's unhealthy to be sick, it hurts to be in pain, and serious illness is no joke. So everyone wants to maximize their wellness.

That's why exercise is so important. Yet many people fail to exercise, or fail to exercise enough, for the simple reason that almost every workout program is bothersome, inconvenient, and exhausting. Are those people therefore doomed to a life of unwellness? Not necessarily!

Happily, there is an alternative to traditional, unappealing techniques of exercise. It's called "Worrycise®," and it makes use of the worrying you normally do anyway to produce beneficial cardiovascular health benefits and firm, toned muscles. Worrying creates not only a calorie-burning effect (as discussed in the previous chapter) but also actual gross physiological changes in one's actual gross physiology.

Impossible? Think back to the last time you were shuddering with terror. Didn't it employ every muscle in your body, as well as stomach, jaws, and sphincters? Wasn't it exhilaratingly fatiguing? Didn't you feel wonderful when it was (finally) over? And didn't it bestow a sense of dignity and importance that "sweating to the oldies" or staggering around a gym cannot approach?

Unfortunately, though, most people cannot simply start vibrating with gut-clenching fear whenever they feel like doing a little exercise. Much of the time our lives just aren't that terrifying. We can, however, learn to cultivate terror's milder, more benign sibling worry, to create a convenient and effective exercise regimen.

A surprisingly wide range of aerobic and isometric benefits can be obtained from everyday worries. After all, we're worried about something, if not many things, all the time. Why, then, don't our bodies reflect this by looking lean, flexed, and fabulous?

Because we engage in *denial*. We deny that we're worried—to others, and to ourselves. Such blatant pretense, ignoring our true feelings and claiming unconcern when in fact we're consumed with concern, is part of the Puritan/Jewish heritage. When someone asks "What's the matter?" we reply either "Nothing" (Puritan) or "Don't ask" (Jewish). Neither response allows us to completely experience the healthful, toning benefits of freely expressed, fully embodied worrying.

That's why the first step to peak physical fitness is to admit, to yourself and to others, that you're worried. In fact, you're worried sick—about some things, or a few things, or about everything. Only then will you feel free enough to practice the pacing, shuddering, tensing, panting, and other Worrycising® movements that can deliver flexed muscles, toned internal organs, and healthful, glowing fingertips.

Worrycise® Benefits

Activity	Worry	Benefit
PACING Steady, continuous walking around room, either back and forth or in circle	Finances; love and/or sex; outcome of important pro sports game	Tones leg muscles; provides mild cardio-pulmonary workout; flexes hips, ankles
SHUDDERING Rapid vibration of torso and/or head; twitching of arms	Street crime; spread of new plagues; fear of not getting enough exercise	Tones torso (back muscles, pectorals); flexes shoulders; strengthens triceps; firms neck muscles
PANTING Heavy, rapid respiration	Perversity of one's sexual fantasies; imminent financial ruin; danger to loved ones; tax audit	Strengthens cardio-pulmonary system; causes perspiration, which flushes skin; tones stomach muscles
NAIL BITING or nibbling at fingernails, pencils and pens, tops of sports bottles	Pending medical test results; kid's pending school acceptances; pending job review	Improves biting aim; strengthens lips and jaw
HAND-WRINGING Clenching hands separately or squeezing hands together in anguish, fear	Missing pets, teenagers, wallet, keys; cute guy/girl doesn't call; cute guy/girl does call, but you say wrong thing	Flexes, strengthens hand muscles, finger muscles, wrists
TOSSING AND TURNING Flopping, rolling over in bed while trying to sleep	Job status; financial status; overall status; big test; upcoming surgical/dental procedure	Twists, flexes, strengthens all major muscle groups; if done rapidly, can provide aerobic workout
STOMACH CHURNING Rhythmic tensing and releasing of stomach, abdominal muscles	Boss's rage; spouse's or lover's anger; parents' fury; police car in rearview mirror	Toughens stomach lining; clears intestines; stomach acid may flush out esophagus

Worrycising® Workouts
Where and When You Want

There is one prerequisite to enjoying the healthful, invigorating effects of Worrycising®, and it applies without exception: *You have to be worried about something.*

But what if you're not? What if, in your daily life, you simply are not stressed or anxious or fearful or nervous? (Note: If you have none of these symptoms, you may be dead. Consult your healthcare professional.) What if you don't go around pacing, shuddering, panting, nail biting, hand wringing, tossing and turning, and stomach churning? What if you're just not worried about anything?

Fortunately this disadvantage is not insurmountable. There are a number of things you can do, practically anywhere and virtually for free, to banish those feelings of happiness, contentment, and security and get yourself good and worried. They range from the mildly annoying to the totally petrifying and so can provide the full spectrum of Worrycising® benefits.

How to Find Something to Worry About

1. **Read the newspaper.**
   Look at the front page and editorial page only.

2. **Call your mother.**
   Or talk to any relative who insists they "only want what's best for you."

3. **Call a miserable friend.**
   Focus on how you are unable to solve their problem.

4. **Watch TV news.**
   Avoid sports and weather.

5. **Join an organization.**
Any group, club, or society will do, since they all thrive on anxiety—that's what gets people to join.

6. **Subscribe to worrisome publications.**
Weekly news magazines and specialty journals are effective.

7. **Stare in the mirror.**
Check for signs of aging, loss of beauty, and malignancies.

8. **Read fashion/lifestyle magazines.**
Realize that you're not beautiful, rich, or famous, and that you're wasting your life reading fashion magazines.

9. **Check your bank balance.**
Compare with total credit card balances, mortgage, utility bills, and all other debt.

10. **Check your investments.**
Compare with value in 1999.

11. **Review your to-do lists.**
Dwell on things still not done.

12. **Read a first-year medical school textbook.**
Find at least two diseases for each of your current symptoms.

13. **Search for indications of what people really think of you.**
Are your phone calls not returned? Are you now invited to fewer parties than you were? Are people being artificially nice?

14. **Admit that you're not in a healthy relationship.**
Ask yourself "Is this the way it's always going to be?"

15. **Ask yourself if you really want to raise children in this world.**
    Reflect on man's inhumanity to man, ongoing pollution, and the essential meaninglessness of life.

16. **Ask yourself if you really want to raise children in *any* world.**
    Consider the costs of food, clothing, shelter, education, and the endless annoyance and ultimate ingratitude of children.

17. **Think about how secure your job really is.**
    Come up with at least two signs that indicate you might be laid off soon.

18. **Ask yourself who is really looking out for you.**
    What would happen if you were injured in a car accident or fell ill? Would anyone take care of you and your family?

Accessorize Your Worrycising®

Looking good goes hand in hand with feeling good, and so it must be avoided at all costs. Choose your Worrycise® apparel and gear accordingly.

Wear clothes that afford the least protection and comfort for the worrying being performed: too few clothes when it's cold, too many when it's hot, and scratchy wool anytime, especially if you're allergic to it. Take special care to find shoes that are one size too small or two sizes too big. Make sure your workout bag contains the following items:

- Old, ill-fitting sweat pants. Must have worn-out, saggy elastic waist band and missing drawstring. Should be depressing to look at indoors and out, under any lighting conditions.

- Old sweatshirt, zip-up or pullover. Hood is optional but pockets are essential for plunging hands into while contracting into a hopeless, despairing ball.

- Woolen socks, unmatching, with visible moth holes.

- Crummy, exhausted headband, inelastic and saggy. Signals, to self and others, that "nothing works."

- Pulse-monitoring wristwatch with loud audio monitor signal. Incessant beep reminds you that a) your life is ticking away and b) that ticking could stop at any moment.

- AM/FM/CD/cassette player. Only AM function should work; earpiece should be broken. Use to listen to news, stock market reports, traffic updates, commercials.

- Shoe or wrist pouch. Forget to put house keys or money into it, providing for a bonus jolt of worry later.

Worrycising® Don'ts
Don't:

- decide that there's nothing you can do about a given topic, or conclude that there's no use worrying about it.

- rush, cheat, or cut short a worrying workout session. Worrying fully with maximum distress and avoiding looking on the bright side will ensure maximum benefits from your worrying sessions.

- forget to frown. Frowning, which exercises important facial muscles, deepens lines and grooves and provides that much more to worry about the next time you look in a mirror.

Worrycising® Competitions

For dedicated worriers and those interested in testing their Worrycising® skills against others in a formal competitive setting, the following events are held annually. Spend a lot of time and money traveling to these events. Then enter the competitions, try hard, lose—and feel great. No complain, no gain!

Bern, Switzerland
World Anxiety Championships,
January 23

Tel Aviv, Israel
Kvetchfest Invitational,
February 12

Sydney, Australia
Semi-Annual No Worries Vs.
Big Worries Nail-Bite-Off,
March 1

San Francisco, USA
North American Secret Fear
Association "Uh-Oh" Games,
March 4–7

Caracas, Venezuela
International Second-
Thought Tournament,
April 2–4

Rio De Janeiro, Brazil
Pan-American Hand-
Wringing Finals,
April 12

Montreal, Canada
North American
Chain-Smoking Finals,
April 16–17

New York City, USA
International Indoor
Shuddering Championship,
May 23

Quito, Ecuador
World Stomach-
Churning Association
Annual Churn-Off,
June 4

Paris, France
Tour d'Ennui de France,
July 7

Frankfurt, Germany
World 15K Pace-Grimace-
and-Sigh Iron Person Invitational,
July 16–18

Djakarta, Indonesia
Southern Hemisphere Talking-to-
Yourself Championship,
August 1–4

London, England
Semi-Annual Vague Unease and
Mounting Disquiet Federation
Brood-Off,
September 12–15

Cairo, Egypt
World Hopelessness Games,
October 5–10

Turin, Italy
Turin Tossing and Turning
Tourney,
October 12–14

Kyoto, Japan
International Perturbation
Games and Folk-Panic Festival,
November 3–7

Rotterdam, The Netherlands
International 10K
Euro-Angst Pairs Tournament,
November 22–24

Oslo, Norway
Despair-Luge
Invitational Finals,
December 2–4

Lagos, Nigeria
Pan-African
Deep-Concern-Off,
December 27

Buenos Aires, Argentina
International Society of Worried
Persons Year-End DreadFest,
December 30–January 2

CAREER MANAGEMENT

Worry at Work to Win!

Everybody worries at work.

That's what work is for—it's an activity you get paid to worry about. Every workplace is the equivalent of a small cogeneration power plant, churning out worry energy (*wergs*) as a by-product of whatever else it produces. And these wergs can really mount up: an average office of twenty-five workers generates enough worry energy in a single eight-hour day to keep the entire population of Buffalo, New York, fretting mildly for a month!

And yet, tragically, most worrying that occurs in the workplace simply burns up worry energy to no good purpose. That huge output of wergs is *almost entirely wasted*. Why? Because most worry at work is worry *about* work—unmanaged, unfocused anxiety about a project, a problem, a colleague, or an account. Just as worrying about your weight does nothing to help you lose pounds, worrying about work accomplishes nothing for your career. Nor does it bring any joy, because there's no need to continue worrying once the problem has been solved.

The workday routine is a model of inefficiency and waste. You worry. You deal with it. You do your job. At the end of the day, you go home, with nothing except worn nerves and a sense of futility and fatigue.

It doesn't have to be this way. You can transform worry from a symptom of workday stress into a useful tool for self-advancement, from a necessary evil into a secret weapon. By worrying properly, you can utilize the power of all that fretting to enhance your image among your coworkers and your superiors, subvert your rivals, control who gets credit (and blame!) for which ideas, and manipulate your boss to give you better assignments, faster promotions, and more money.

Enhance Your Stature: Worry as Makeover

As the following chart demonstrates, careful worrying *out loud* about selected *nonwork* topics can enhance your image in a number of areas. Moreover, note that competence at your job is entirely unnecessary. You needn't be able to solve problems, propose innovations, or even know the difference between a Post-It and a Power Point.

Let others make themselves miserable striving for excellence and seeking creative, practical solutions to professional challenges. Focus *your* worrying so that it concerns not your job but the outside world. Rather than suffer anxiety over the Maxwell contract (about which you know nothing), convey your leadership qualities by redirecting that worry to world events that are as familiar to others (whom you wish to impress) as they are to yourself.

Add your own topics to those in the chart. Just make sure that a) you pick generally familiar subjects of national or world scope, but not any that you might be expected to actually do anything about, and b) others hear you. Your aim should be to look good to people who can help you, not to agonize in private.

Diminish the Status of Others: Subversive Worrying

One way to better your own fortune at work is to bring down someone else's fortune. And there's no better way to do this than to make

Enhance Your Stature

Effect	*Concern*	*Sample*

"Voter participation is declining. What happens if nobody shows up to vote? Do we just go back to a monarchy?"

National elections

DECISIVENESS

"The genie's out of the bottle. Sooner or later something monstrous is going to happen."

Recombinant DNA, cloning

FORESIGHT

"It's the Eskimos I'm worried about. They have 17 words for 'snow' but no word for 'petro-chemical sludge'."

Drilling for oil in Alaska

PEOPLE SKILLS, EMPATHY

"Pretty soon nobody will be able to afford college. Why can't we have a Sam's Club University?"

Rising university tuition

INNOVATION

"It's a great technology, but I'm worried that it's in danger because nobody's buying it. They should apply it to security cameras. Wouldn't it be great to finally look good on the TV at the 7-Eleven?"

Conversion to digital television

CREATIVITY

subtle negative implications about them cloaked in the seemingly innocent guise of your own petty worries. The principle here is indirectness: never criticize the target of your campaign directly. (It might cause others to disagree with you and *praise* your rival and, besides, it isn't nice.) Instead, learn to work damaging innuendos about your enemy into what seem to be routine complaints about your own personal problems.

In the examples in the chart, the hypothetical colleague you wish to destroy will be called Ed. Be sure to make all these comments in a tone of genial, disinterested seriousness, without malice or cattiness. If Ed himself shows up, show great admiration for him.

Wisdom About Worry from Ancient China

The strategic use of worrying to advance one's career is nothing new. Long before the invention of the nasty rumor, the ancients understood how worrying, if employed with discipline and awareness, could serve as a means to thwart one's enemies, appropriate their ideas as one's own, and curry favor with the emperor.

The following three excerpts are taken from the ancient Chinese text known as *The Art of the Vexatious*. Thought to have been written and circulated around 460 B.C., it became the basis of the universally practiced martial art Tai Kwan D'uh-oh. The book takes the form of a series of poetic epigrams addressed to a warlord, whom the author refers to as "Noble Worrier." The work is attributed to Wung Li, a scholar and philosopher. An explanatory annotation follows each extract.

To Obtain and Possess the Ideas of Others

O Noble Worrier, treat the Ideas of Others as the unruly children of unfit parents. Worry about them, adopt them, correct them, and they will be yours.

Diminish the Stature of Others

If you want your enemy to seem	then worry about	to	and say,
LAZY	your cuticles	your mutual boss	"I'm chewing my fingernails up with anxiety over these three new projects I've taken on. Meanwhile, check out Ed's. He's got nails like a hand model."
INCOMPETENT	computer games	your mutual coworkers	"I love Super Pinball, but with all these assignments, I never get a chance to practice! I'll never play as well as Ed."
DISHONEST	your appearance	your mutual coworkers or boss	"Do my shoes look OK? Ed said they looked great, but you know him. He'll say anything."
IRRESPONSIBLE	Post-working-lunch sleepiness	your mutual boss	"I only had a salad and I'm afraid I'm going to pass out. Meanwhile, Ed had the prime rib and mashed potatoes. I don't know how he manages to stay awake!"

When a business rival voices an idea you wish to appropriate as your own, greet it with a great deal of worry—about its cost, effectiveness, drain on resources, and so on. When he replies to your concerns, wave off his comments and tell him, "Nah, that won't do it." Then volunteer to deal with the "problems" yourself. Later, report back that you have solved the problems (many of which never really existed) and are ready to continue from there. You will by then own the idea and be credited for it in the minds of others.

To Manipulate and Impress One's Superior

O Noble Worrier, be not afraid to employ Worry as a Sword. Are not the Mighty as susceptible to the blade as the Meek? Then wield or withhold Vexatiating thus.

Use worry as a sword to scare your boss. Express fears about whatever is going on, taking care to first feel out your superior for what scares him or her the most. Then, later, soothe your boss's fears by announcing that you've determined there's nothing to worry about. The more you learn to identify your boss's unique, personal weaknesses, the better you'll be able to alternately frighten and calm your boss. Soon you'll become, in your boss's mind, terrifying—and indispensable.

To Protect Oneself from Blame and Contumely

O Noble Worrier, how best to avoid besmirchment, when the dung strikes the spinning pinwheel? Let Worry be your shield. He who has Artfully Vexated about every possible peril, and done so openly and in the face of one and all, is surely exempt from Blame.

To avoid getting in trouble, worry—publicly and loudly—about every possible issue up front. Worry thus becomes a shield, protecting you from blame when things go wrong, since you've already gone on record expecting the worst.

Neutralize Others: Worry as Flak

Sooner or later your rivals are going to have ideas as good as or better than yours, assuming you ever have any. When this happens, don't just stand worriedly by and watch them triumph, winning accolades from peers, impressing the boss, and actually earning promotions. Instead, give free rein to your strongest impulses to worry and fear, sending up a barrage of seemingly relevant counter-ideas that will leave your competitor's notions in shreds. All people will remember is the eloquence and cogency—and constancy—of your criticism, not the merits (or even the source!) of the underlying proposal.

For example, let us assume your enemy presents ideas at a staff meeting. How can you deflate these threatening initiatives and inflate your own importance? It's simple:

1. Always begin your response with, "I can't believe we're seriously discussing this" (even if you're the one who brought it up).

2. Concede that maybe the idea "has a place," but not now, and not for this purpose.

3. Present a strong, firm counterargument. Assemble your argument from one, or dozens, of the following Concern-O-Matic selections.

Concern-O-Matic

Beginning with Step 1, create a compelling, if opaque, argument by adding on selections from the following pattern, in order. (See table, "Concern-O-Matic," pages 44–45.) Repeat the idea you're attacking, and then say, in tones of selfless concern and informed worry:

Concern-O-Matic

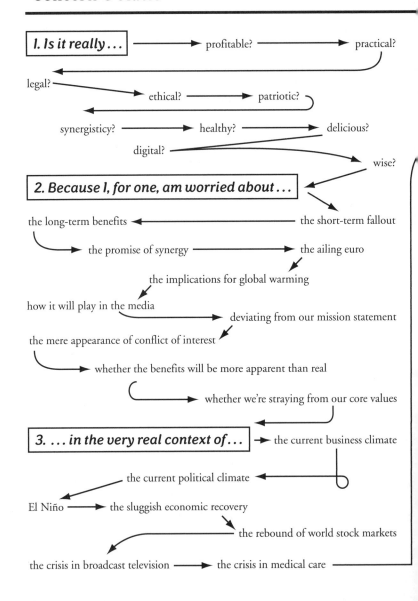

1. Is it really... ➝ profitable? ➝ practical?

legal? ➝ ethical? ➝ patriotic?

synergisticy? ➝ healthy? ➝ delicious?

digital? ➝ wise?

2. Because I, for one, am worried about...

the long-term benefits ⬅ the short-term fallout

the promise of synergy ➝ the ailing euro

the implications for global warming

how it will play in the media ➝ deviating from our mission statement

the mere appearance of conflict of interest

whether the benefits will be more apparent than real

whether we're straying from our core values

3. ... in the very real context of... ➝ the current business climate

the current political climate ⬅

El Niño ➝ the sluggish economic recovery

the rebound of world stock markets

the crisis in broadcast television ➝ the crisis in medical care

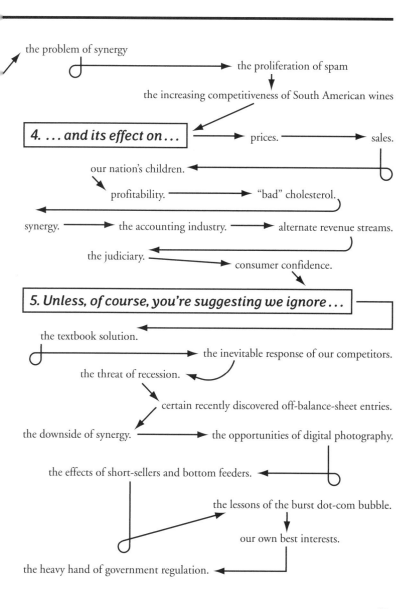

the problem of synergy

the proliferation of spam

the increasing competitiveness of South American wines

4. ... and its effect on ... prices. sales.

our nation's children.

profitability. "bad" cholesterol.

synergy. the accounting industry. alternate revenue streams.

the judiciary. consumer confidence.

5. Unless, of course, you're suggesting we ignore ...

the textbook solution.

the inevitable response of our competitors.

the threat of recession.

certain recently discovered off-balance-sheet entries.

the downside of synergy. the opportunities of digital photography.

the effects of short-sellers and bottom feeders.

the lessons of the burst dot-com bubble.

our own best interests.

the heavy hand of government regulation.

Offer to Help Your Rivals:
Worry as Misdirection

The advice offered previously promotes certain tactics that some might deem underhanded. But what if you're someone for whom active subversion or character assassination is just too violent? What if you just can't find it in yourself to be ruthless? Can you still use worrying to impede your adversaries and advance yourself?

Yes, and the technique is simple: merely volunteer to worry about (and, implicitly, to solve) any problem about which your enemy (let's call him Ed) complains. No matter what Ed agonizes about, say to him, "You let me worry about that, Ed."

Then really do worry about it. But do nothing else. Consult no one. Offer no solutions. Don't actually *think* about it. Just worry. If Ed asks about it, merely repeat, "You let me worry about that, Ed." And pretty much just sit on it until, one day, the roof caves in—on top of Ed.

In this way, worry is used as a form of magic, much as a stage magician will direct your attention to one thing while manipulating other things. When your focus returns to the original object, it has—impossibly—changed. It's "magic." Thus, by taking the focus off Ed, and then returning it to him, you've deftly transformed him from a capable, respected worker to someone who is seen as lazy and unreliable. You've fooled him—and your boss—all with the power of worry.

PERSONAL FINANCE

Worry Your Way to Wealth!

Are you making money? Is your money making money? Is the money your money is making making as much money as it could? If you're like most people, your answer to the above is "Leave me alone."

Acquiring wealth, investing it, saving it, protecting it, planning for retirement: these are daunting tasks, involving complex factors and esoteric knowledge most of us simply don't have. So we turn to those who supposedly do have it—and run smack into the Financial Advisor Paradox: "If my financial advisor is so smart, what's he doing working for me as a financial advisor? Why isn't he financially advising himself and already rich?"

It's enough to make you worry about your money and its ability to make more money for you to worry about. But this would be a mistake. True, money and worrying were made for each other. But the way to worry your way to wealth is not by worrying about making money, but by worrying about *everything else in the world*. So stop worrying *about* making money and start worrying *to* make money!

The Power of Assertive Fretting

During the boom years of the late 1990s a shocking fact came to light in the world of finance: securities brokers and investment counselors often reserve the hottest new issues at the lowest prices for their favored clients. Stock brokers play favorites! It's appalling, outrageous, disgusting, disgraceful, and possibly illegal, and your reaction when you truly grasp the significance of this fact should be to demand, How can I get in on it?

Through worrying, of course, but not the internalized, hand-wringing kind. Instead, you'll need to worry "at" a particular person. We call this outer-directed worrying by various names: "badgering," "noodging," "pestering," "nagging," "harassing," and "stalking," to name a few. They differ in nuance and degree of criminality, but they mean essentially the same thing: subjecting *someone else* to your own personal worry processes.

Such a strategy can prove surprisingly effective when you are trying to persuade a financial advisor to share his most treasured secrets. By impressing upon the advisor the depth and urgency of your investment concerns—by sharing your worries with him openly, sincerely, and relentlessly—you increase the chances that he'll cut you in on a special offering.

Worry Your Way onto Your Broker's A-List

1. Put his office number on your speed dial. Use it all the time—every time you make a call. When you call out for pizza, call him first. When he answers, ask him for pizza. When he says, "We're an investment service, not a pizza parlor," remind him that you're still waiting for some of those insider stock picks.

2. During off-hours, try his cell phone. Keep trying.

3. Leave detailed messages when he doesn't answer.

4. Call him at home. Tell him you're worried that he's forgotten you.

5. If members of his family answer, share your worries with them. Win their respect (and possibly their help) by soliciting their opinions. See if his wife has any insights into T-bills. Ask his children about derivatives. Learn, and use, their names.

6. When you get him on the phone, ask him for his take on information you've picked up on-line, from colleagues in the office, or from strangers at the ballpark. Subscribe to all the investment magazines and ask him if he is for or against every recommendation you find in them.

7. Tell him that you are uncertain about the direction of the Dow, the Fed, the prime, the dollar, the yen, the euro, OPEC, Fannie Mae, Freddie Mac, and everything else, and that you want to know what he thinks. Keep expressing your concerns until he asks, "What do you want from me?"

8. Explain to him that you'd sleep a lot easier, have fewer questions, and call him a lot less, if he put your money into something "special," something new and fresh and clean.

9. If he claims not to know what you're talking about, apologize. Blame yourself. Tell him it just shows you're confused and need his help. Reiterate the intensity of your concern.

10. Keep calling (return to step 1).

11. Watch how fast you get those "special" offers.

Insurance: Beyond Life and Auto

Insurance, an essential tool for preserving and increasing wealth, is nothing more than worry that puts its money where its mouth is. Society's concerns have expanded since the old days of home-life-auto, and the insurance industry has kept pace. Following are seven groundbreaking products that reflect the new priorities and concerns of the rich and worried. Let your worry guide you to obtain the proper policies—and big payouts!

1. Endumpment protection. Awards policy holder cash benefit if he or she is dumped by girl- or boyfriend. *Whole endumpment* is payable in lump-sum premium, accumulates cash value as reltionship continues, and may be redeemed upon marriage. *Term endumpment* is a pay-as-you-go policy, with no cash value buildup.

2. Fertility protection. Provides lump-sum or annuity pay-out if fertility drugs bring conception of two or more babies. Complex actuarial tables plotting number-of-babies versus funds-needed-to-support-family versus odds-of-conception requires expert counseling before purchase of plan. (Also available is *infertility insurance*, compensating couples unable to conceive, either with or without fertility drugs, and who therefore had all that sex for nothing.)

3. Divorce insurance. Available to both husband and wife, each covered separately. Premarital counseling discounts are available in most areas. Payout schedule, pegged to length of marriage, means benefit exceeds premium only after third anniversary.

4. Summer house insurance. Compensates insured person in the event individuals he or she shares a summer house with are idiots. Riders are available to cover housemates' or guests' breakage, vandalism, destruction of garbage disposal by insertion of

lobster shells and/or corn cobs, and unnecessary exploding of toilets. Note: Coverage does not include bad weather; neighbors who are idiots; or personal injury due to drinking, sunburn, or reckless behavior.

5. College graduate fecklessness compensation. Pays lump sum to parent(s) or legal guardian(s) of student who graduates from accredited college or university and is just as much a poky, drifting, directionless ninny as when he or she entered. Supplemental coverage is available in the event of postgraduate return of student to live in policy holder's primary residence.

6. General inconvenience indemnification. "Blanket" or "umbrella" coverage against loss of time and/or money, or for incursion of distress, annoyance, and/or irritation due to general inconveniences of contemporary life, including but not limited to air travel problems (long lines, bad food, unpleasant seat neighbor), computer malfunction, deteriorating memory, restaurant outrages (rude service, bad food, etc.), entrapment in institutional or corporate voice-mail system, and more. Expensive.

7. Insurance insurance. Compensates policy holder for having purchased various insurance policies (at least five) that have never paid off, due to absence of accident, disaster, mishap, or death.

The Worried Person's Portfolio

The smart investor knows that the most important principle for creating a successful financial plan is to diversify—to invest in a variety of investment vehicles such as stocks, bonds, mutual funds, commodities, Treasury bills, certificates of deposit, and real estate investment trusts (REITs). Then, if certain sectors of the economy begin to struggle, the losses incurred in one part of the portfolio are

The Worried Portfolio

Smart Diversification: Sample Portfolio Ranked
by Percentage of Total Investment

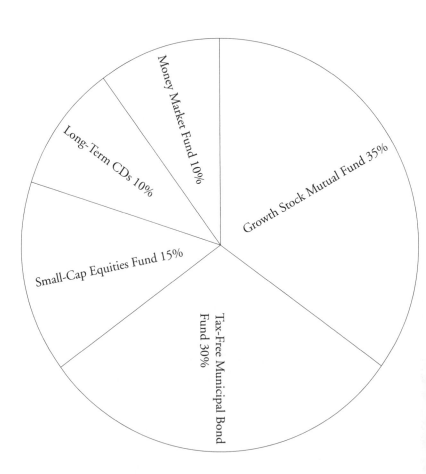

Terror-Based Diversification: Sample Portfolio Ranked by Percentage of Total Investment

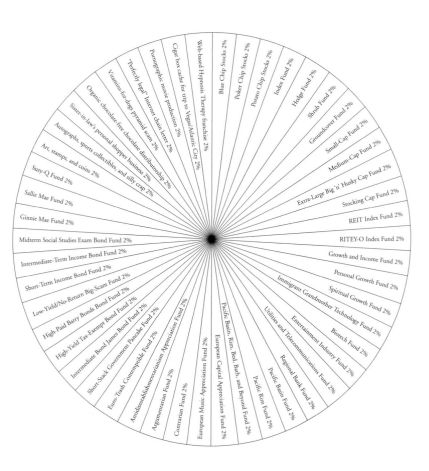

Web-based Hypnosis Therapy franchise 2%
Blue Chip Stocks 2%
Poker Chip Stocks 2%
Potato Chip Stocks 2%
Index Fund 2%
Hedge Fund 2%
Shrub Fund 2%
Groundcover Fund 2%
Small-Cap Fund 2%
Medium-Cap Fund 2%
Extra-Large Big 'n' Husky Cap Fund 2%
Stocking Cap Fund 2%
REIT Index Fund 2%
RITEY-O Index Fund 2%
Growth and Income Fund 2%
Personal Growth Fund 2%
Spiritual Growth Fund 2%
Immigrant Grandmother Technology Fund 2%
Biotech Fund 2%
Entertainment Industry Fund 2%
Utilities and Telecommunications Fund 2%
Regional Bank Fund 2%
Pacific Basin Fund 2%
Pacific Rim Fund 2%
Pacific Basin, Rim, Bed, Bath, and Beyond Fund 2%
European Capital Appreciation Fund 2%
European Music Appreciation Fund 2%
Contrarian Fund 2%
Argumentarian Fund 2%
Antidisestablishmentarianism Appreciation Fund 2%
Euro-Trash Contemptible Fund 2%
Short-Stack Government Pancake Fund 2%
Intermediate Bond James Bond Fund 2%
High-Yield Tax-Exempt Bond Fund 2%
High-Paid Barry Bonds Bond Fund 2%
Low-Yield/No-Return Big-Scam Fund 2%
Short-Term Income Bond Fund 2%
Intermediate-Term Income Bond Fund 2%
Midterm Social Studies Exam Bond Fund 2%
Ginnie Mae Fund 2%
Sallie Mae Fund 2%
Suzy-Q Fund 2%
Art, stamps, and coins 2%
Autographs, sports collectibles, and silly crap 2%
Sister-in-law's personal shopper business 2%
Organic chocolate-free chocolate distributorship 2%
Vitamins-for-dogs pyramid scam 2%
"Perfectly legal" Internet chain letter 2%
Pornographic movie production 2%
Cigar box cache for trip to Vegas/Atlantic City 2%

made up for by gains in another. Diversifying is what makes the smart investor smart.

But the worried investor knows that it's not enough to be smart. It's better to be smart *and terrified*. That's why the worried investor seeks not just Smart Diversification, but Terror-Based Diversification. By not only acknowledging the possibility of bad economic news but by actively anticipating it, the worried investor is always prepared.

Say the Dow plunges 6 percent in three months. The smart investor might take that as a wakeup call—to suddenly question the wisdom of making stocks the dominant part of his portfolio. And so he might give closer scrutiny to other forms of investment.

But the worried investor never needs a wakeup call—because he never sleeps. He's always awake, always fearing the worst, and investing accordingly. The worried investor never has to suddenly question the wisdom of anything, because he lives in a perpetual state of questioning the wisdom of everything. The worried investor never has to stop to think about other forms of investment, because her portfolio consists of a little bit of every possible form already.

The reader may be thinking, "Well, I'm smart, and I may even be a little worried. But how can I learn to be terrified?" The principle is simple: devote thirty minutes a week to at least Moderate Stewing on your portfolio, your retirement fund, or the financial news of the day. By the eighteen-minute mark you'll realize, with a plunging sense of nauseated terror, that you don't understand the slightest thing about the world of investments.

You don't really know what makes the stock market go up or down, why a company can report good news and then have its stock drop, or why a company can report quarterly losses and then have its stock soar. You'll look at two-hundred-point swings in the Dow with the blank perplexity of a child watching a chess match. It will occur to you viscerally that your economic solvency and financial future are in the hands of strangers who operate in ways you cannot fathom or trust.

You're worried and frightened and you want nothing more than to not have to think about the whole thing. And yet you feel you must.

This is the moment when you're ready for Terror-Based Diversification. You'll be willing (indeed, eager) to spread out the risk and uncertainty of investment—and the sheer, heart-pounding fear of it—among not three or four or five investment vehicles but thirty or forty or fifty.

Admittedly, it's complicated. Investing in fifty different companies or funds means reviewing numerous graphs of value and return, and receiving box loads of prospectuses and corporate reports that you can hardly be bothered to recycle, let alone read (forget "understand").

And that is one of the key elements of Terror-Based Diversity: you make your own investment portfolio so complicated and overwhelming that it becomes unnecessary—or, really, impossible—to think about it at all. Isn't that almost like having peace of mind? (See "The Worried Portfolio," pages 54–55 for sample portfolios.)

The Worrier's Hot Prospect List: Five Growth Areas for Short- and Medium-Term Investment

Occasionally it's important to stop worrying about ourselves and our investments, look outward at the world around us, and ask what other people are worried about. New businesses will arise to service society's new worries, and we want to anticipate them. Why? Because we care about society, and we care about new business growth, and we very much want to make a killing in them.

Here (see page 58) are some hot areas of worry that will, over the next ten years, generate significant opportunities for businesses. Find those companies, invest in them today, and worry all the way to the bank.

1. **SUV-envy retrofitting.** Drivers of conventional vehicles will feel increasingly intimidated by and jealous of sport utility vehicles (SUVs). A new industry will offer bulging side panels, ultra-large tires, and other accessories to make ordinary cars look like SUVs.

2. **SUV-shame retrofitting.** As backlash builds against the environmental and safety dangers posed by SUVs, many owners will want to disguise their behemoths and escape societal censure. Look for companies offering oversize windshield wipers, roof racks, and gas tank caps, and undersize tires, to make giant vehicles seem smaller.

3. **Sports ticket financial services.** Baseball, basketball, football, and soccer salaries are skyrocketing, while luxury-box stadiums are being built to coddle corporate clients. The result: ticket prices increase exponentially. Storefront and on-line lenders offering to finance the purchase of tickets to sporting events will soon become a necessity for the middle-class fan willing to incur short-term debt in his desperation for a couple of passes to the game.

4. **A nation forgets.** As the Baby Boom generation ages, look for more and more forgetting of more and more names, facts, and song lyrics, creating a need for prompting and reminding on a national scale. Service companies with names like Little Birdie, Inc., Still Small Voice, Inc., and Friendly Reminder, Inc. will find and fill this need, sending daily e-mail reminders, making scheduled, preemptive phone calls (e.g., "Good morning, Mister Smith. Today's reminder: The actress you've always liked but can never remember the name of is *Dame Judi Dench* . . . "), and providing in-ear transceivers connected to a central office. When the client stammers forgetfully, a staff member

responds, broadcasting on a private frequency the needed name, fact, locker combination, movie title, or spousal endearment.

5. **Over-the-counter placebos.** The costs of prescription drugs and health care are already high and getting higher. The solution? Placebos—sugar pills used in blind drug tests that often prove nearly as effective as the drug itself but cost far less. Brand name or generic, these placebo pills, syrups, patches, and suppositories "do no harm" and just might do some good.

Market Trend Worry

If you're worried about ...	then consider investing in ...
GLOBAL WARMING	Manufacturers of air conditioners without CFCs; sports drinks companies; Norwegian fjord cruise lines; all-ice hotel developers
CARPAL TUNNEL SYNDROME	Doorknob research firms; wrist rest, splint manufacturers; precooked meals, take-out food container companies; modular units that convert kitchens into closets
DIMINISHMENT OF CIVILITY IN EVERYDAY LIFE	Taser, pepper spray, stun-gun research; gated-community development; earplug and eyeshade manufacturers
AGING PARENTS	Retirement community development; louder headphone and speaker technology; faster wheelchairs; cloning
THE AIRLINE INDUSTRY	Smaller, regional carriers; maglev trains; video-conferencing technology
INCREASE IN PLAGIARISM	Polygraph technology; ethics-instructional video production; Google, if it ever goes public

Worrier, Know Thyself

Finding out what other people are worried about is a sound investment strategy, but don't overlook your own concerns. You can, and should, invest in them, too.

Trust your worry. Believe in it. Most likely, if you're worried about something, so are a lot of people. You can bemoan this fact as somehow threatening to your sense of "specialness"—or you can exploit it for significant financial gains.

Start by getting a sheet of paper and making a list of the things you're most worried about, most passionate about, and most frightened of, and the things you most anxiously dread. That's where the opportunities will be.

DATING

He Frets, She Frets

Worrying and dating have been inseparable since the dawn of time.

How could it be otherwise? Dating is the method by which we check out or audition or "product test" candidates with whom we feel we might fall in love, with whom we might have babies, with whom we might live for a long time. And they do the same with us. Dating is our society's way of perpetuating the eternal, universal human experiences of mate selection, procreation, child rearing, separation, divorce, and property settlement.

Our very survival, as individuals, as a culture, and as a species, is thus based on our ability to date. No wonder we worry! And no wonder date worry is so complex.

There are three separate stages of date worry: before, during, and after a date.

Date Worry by Stage

BEFORE

Worry	Action	Benefit
Of asking someone out on a date face to face	Calling, e-mailing, or writing	Promotes growth in telecommunications, computer, Internet, on-line dating industries; fuels digital revolution; transforms society
Of offending date with poor personal hygiene	Showering, shaving, using deodorant	Results in healthy, pleasant environment
Of seeming like slob	Wearing clean clothes; ironing shirt	Shows respect for date and others; supports dry cleaners
Of alienating date by being tardy	Showing up on time	Supports auto, mass transit, wristwatch industries
Of being considered unattractive	Combing hair, wearing fashionable clothes, smiling, giving compliments and flowers	Makes date and everyone else feel good about themselves; supports fashion, personal grooming, flower industries

DURING

Worry	Action	Benefit
Of not knowing where to go	Asking friends and reading newspapers, books, magazines for ideas	Improves communications; broadens cultural horizons; increases sales of newspapers, books, magazines
Of not knowing how strong to "come on"	Paying exquisite attention to date's moods and receptivity	Shows respect for date's feelings; expands own ability to empathize

Worry	Action	Benefit
Of having sex with wrong person	Encouraging date to talk about him- or herself, listening to date	Avoids mismatching, anger, resentment; promotes satisfaction
Of seeming dumb, passive; of being bored	Being actively charming, interesting, or seductive	Enhances self-respect; enables you to stay awake; entices date
Of getting involved with mean or nasty person, idiot, or jerk	Declining sex until ready	Maintains personal standards; keeps date interested; limits population; creates higher-quality gene pool

AFTER

Worry	Action	Benefit
Of being alone	Calling date the next day, being receptive when called back	Shows respect for date, stability of relationships; boosts mobile phone sales
Of being thought slob	Cleaning apartment or home and clothing for next date	Promotes orderliness and cleanliness; combats entropy
Of not getting sex	Asking for another date	Provides possibility of ongoing relationship
Of not getting married	Asking for or agreeing to another date	Increases possibility of ongoing relationship; reduces therapy bills
Of not having children	Asking for or agreeing to another date	Maximizes possibility of having sex and an ongoing relationship; promotes survival of society and lawyers

The Unworried Worrier

But suppose you're someone who simply isn't worried when asking someone on a date. What if you're supremely confident, or cynically resigned? Can you still take advantage of the magic of worrying?

Certainly. One effective way is to use worry as a means of manipulation, in a kind of moral jujitsu: *Your* worry makes *them* defensive—they suddenly feel ashamed of their unworried, cavalier outlook. It's easy, it works equally well for both men and women, and it enables you to exploit one of the most potent strategies in the entire world of dating—the Power of *No*.

Simply engage in preliminary small talk, as you normally would, to establish the basic connection. If, after a while (between five and thirty minutes), you fail to strike a spark or sense the least bit of chemistry, give up and move on. But if you do seem to be making progress, wait until the next relaxed moment—usually just after a nervous little laugh at some quip by either one of you—and suddenly look regretful, saddened, and apologetic.

Don't even wait to be asked what is wrong. Launch immediately, preemptively, into the Six Steps of Shame. By "confessing" how worried you are about the important things, you'll shame the other person (who is less nobly worried than you) into reaching out and *insisting* that you date him or her.

Here are the six steps, followed by ways to implement them:

Step 1: You state that you'd "really like" to continue the relationship.

Step 2: You admit that, sadly, that would be difficult, because of your current worried state.

Step 3: You lay out specifically what bothers you.

Step 4: You explain what social/dating activity is impeded by your worrying.

Step 5: You demonstrate how it is impeded.

Step 6: You say how he/she can help.

Six Steps of Shame-O-Matic

As long as you take care to use one option from each category from the chart on pages 68–69, in the order given, the options within each are interchangeable. Mix and match and manipulate your worry to achieve dating success!

Put on an Unhappy Face

Once the other person agrees to go on a date with you, you actually have to go on it. Then the real work starts: saying and doing the right thing in order to impress your date.

It's not easy. But it is possible, and worrying can help, no matter what your short- (fun, sex), medium- (fun, sex, love), or long- (fun, sex, love, marriage, children, grandchildren) term dating goals are.

The trick, as always, is to know what or whom to worry about.

Worry to Wow: How to Impress Your Date

For men

Worrying can make a man seem emotionally expressive and intellectually alert, while avoiding the appearance of being weak. Women love it.

Note: As always, the term *worry* used below refers to good worrying. All worrying should attain at least a Brooding intensity and be

Shame-O-Matic

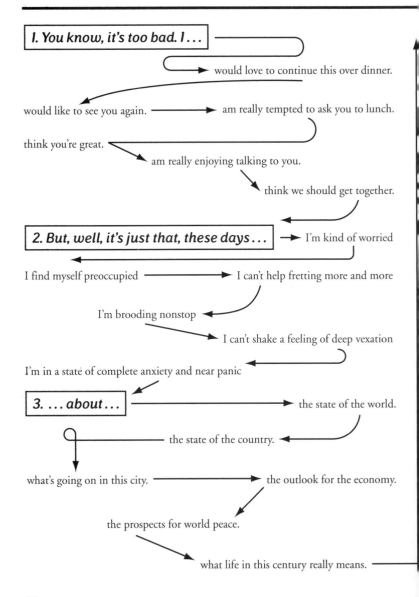

1. You know, it's too bad. I . . .

would love to continue this over dinner.

would like to see you again. — am really tempted to ask you to lunch.

think you're great.

am really enjoying talking to you.

think we should get together.

2. But, well, it's just that, these days . . . — I'm kind of worried

I find myself preoccupied — I can't help fretting more and more

I'm brooding nonstop

I can't shake a feeling of deep vexation

I'm in a state of complete anxiety and near panic

3. . . . about . . . — the state of the world.

the state of the country.

what's going on in this city. — the outlook for the economy.

the prospects for world peace.

what life in this century really means.

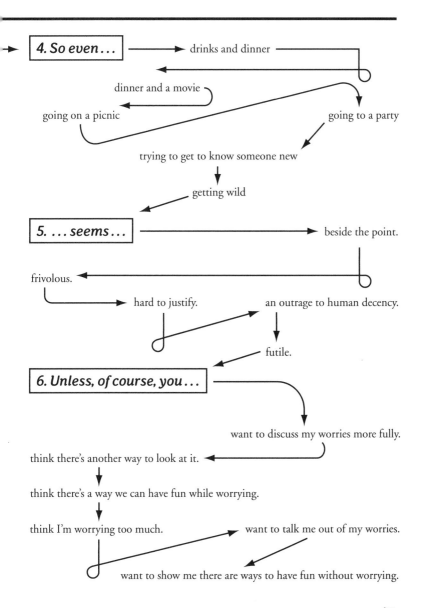

4. So even... → drinks and dinner

dinner and a movie

going on a picnic   going to a party

trying to get to know someone new

getting wild

5. ... seems...   beside the point.

frivolous.

hard to justify.   an outrage to human decency.

futile.

6. Unless, of course, you...

want to discuss my worries more fully.

think there's another way to look at it.

think there's a way we can have fun while worrying.

think I'm worrying too much.   want to talk me out of my worries.

want to show me there are ways to have fun without worrying.

openly discussed when cued by a woman's question, such as "What's wrong?" "What's the matter?" "Is something wrong?" "What are you thinking?" and so on.

In order to seem...

ROMANTIC: *Worry about Fate.* Show concern about how the gods must have some terrible thing in store for you, since they'd never let you get away with meeting someone so wonderful without some compensating blah blah tragic blah.
You say: "I know it's crazy, but I feel like some larger force has brought us together, and it freaks me out."

ARTISTIC: *Worry about the human condition.* Look troubled, pained, and strangely remote. Then talk like a high school poet.
You say: "Starvation, brutality, suffering . . . how can the world that contains all that also contain us, sitting here, sharing pecan pie?" (This can be used whether you're sharing pecan pie with her or not. *Especially* when not—it's more "artistic.")

SENSITIVE: *Worry about her feelings.* Voice concern about about her physical and/or emotional comfort. Mean, or pretend to mean, it.
You say: "That waiter had no right to condescend to you like that."

NEEDY: *Worry about yourself.* Many women fantasize about finding a broken man and fixing him. You can be that broken, pathetic man! When asked why you seem so worried, look devastated and allude to a previous bad romance. Wonder out loud if you can trust her.
You say: "No, nothing's wrong. Just . . . something happened to me, once."

DEEP: *Worry about clichés.* Speak earnestly and with emotion about the kind of big, vague, important-seeming things you'd find in greeting cards.

You say: "There are walls between us. Walls of emotion. Walls of pain. Walls of selfishness. I just worry, sometimes, about being able to climb those walls."

MACHO: *Worry about nothing.* Or at least claim to. Note that you're unworried, not because you're blithely carefree, but because your rugged, stoical strength refuses to acknowledge adversity or fear.

You say: "Look at the men in this restaurant. Have you noticed that they're all worried about something? Poor bastards. They don't know how to live."

EXISTENTIAL: *Worry about worrying.* Wonder about your capacity for wonder; be concerned about your ability to be concerned. Works well with women who talk all the time about their "life."

You say: "Do I worry enough? or too little? I wish I knew."

For women

Unfairly enough, worrying on a date is probably less accepted for women than for men. Women are often expected to provide the warmth and to emotionally expedite a social encounter.

In order to seem ...

SEDUCTIVE: *Worry about his comfort.* To men, especially on a date, anything referring to the sensation of touch is a sexual overture. Use advisedly.

You say: "I was just wondering—is your seat as comfortable as mine?"

INTELLECTUAL: *Worry about ideas.* Apply large abstractions to human society and find the result "troubling." This is an intellectual way of saying "scary" and will keep him from thinking you're all intellect and no heart.

You say: "With the death of Marxism, some people seem to think it is no longer permissible to discuss dialectics. I find that troubling."

INDEPENDENT: *Worry about yourself (but not your feelings).* And do it without complaining. Strive for rueful, good humored comments about having to get along in the world. It'll show him that, when he has bad news (he's sleeping with someone else; he's a wanted fugitive; he's married), you can take it. Like a man.

You say: "Sorry. I was just thinking about killing my boss. Is murder still illegal?"

NURTURING: *Worry about his feelings.* Many men expect this, but (or, rather, therefore) it still works. He wants you to worry about his feelings so he doesn't have to. Just beware of coming on too strong.

You say: "Me? Nothing. I'm not worried. I just thought that you looked worried."

ARTISTIC: *Worry and obsess about something weird.* The artist is assumed to be the hyper-individualist, the one who can afford to embody qualities the rest of us can't. Openly fret about some private, kooky concern.

You say: "How would life be if you could close your ears but not your eyes?"

ROMANTIC: *Worry about your ability to resist him.* The essence of romance is to be overwhelmed. So be, or worry about being, overwhelmed.

You say: "As a matter of fact, I am worried. I'm worried about how I'm going to drag myself away from you tonight and get ready for work tomorrow."

Dating and Worrying On-Line

On-line dating services allow for immediate contact and response via e-mail, and some offer real-time chat. They also make it easy to provide photographs and even brief audio greetings to a world-wide membership of various special interests—professional, Jewish, Christian, divorced, gay, and, of course, worried.

Try Worry-Woo.com or Anxie-Date.com to meet singles who are available and interested in finding that special, worried someone.

Most Popular Movies for Worriers

Desperately Seeking Susan
High Anxiety
The Brood
Panic in Needle Park
Women on the Verge of a Nervous Breakdown
Cape Fear
Panic Room

Most Popular Movie About Not Worrying

Dr. Strangelove or: How I Learned to Stop Worrying and
   Love the Bomb

When You're Turned Down for a Date

Don't take it personally. There are better things to worry about.

#

The Essence of Worry

Sex is to worry as a breeder reactor is to fissionable material. Just as the reactor actually creates more radioactive material than it consumes, so does sex make you more intensely worried, and about more things, than you ever were about having the sex in the first place!

The more sex you have, the more worried you become. But not having any sex can be worrisome, too.

The great pioneer of this understanding was Sigmund Freud. Sexuality, Freud said, was the central engine driving an individual's emotional and psychological life, and therefore the life of a culture. "Everything comes down to sex" was, for decades, the popular shorthand summary of Freud's system, and most educated people believed it.

Today, of course, we know better. We are aware that Freud developed his theories at a time of sexual repression and hypocrisy, and so he quite understandably ended up ascribing to sexuality an undue level of importance. We know that the true central engine of individual and cultural development is not sex, but worry.

Worry, not sex, is what forces us out of bed, makes us get dressed, prompts us to feed the dog and take the kids to school, and compels us to go to work. Then, once we're at work, we invent the sewing machine, compose *The Messiah*, build the cathedral at

Chartres, and do all those other things that civilization is so famous for. We do them because we're worried.

However, it is precisely because worry is so fundamental to the human psyche that it can be used to improve, or obtain, one's sex life.

Get Worried and Be Wonderful

The Anxious Male Lover

When asked what they consider attractive or sexy, many women answer, "Confidence." This, of course, is just what confident men want (and expect) to hear, and hearing it doesn't affect them very much.

But it can have a different effect on unconfident men. If you're one of this group, then hearing that women look for confidence only undercuts what little you have, increasing your sexual anxiety about how you'll perform and trapping you in a self-perpetuating cycle of worry.

You lucky devil!

Why lucky? Because, thanks to the boon of worrying in bed, you become an anxiety machine, generating huge quantities of worry energy you can put to excellent use, pleasing your partner, enjoying yourself, and creating an experience both you and she will, at least for a while, remember always.

Here are five ways to make your bedroom nervousness work for you.

1. Show your nervousness. Tremble slightly as you take off your clothes and hers. Make sure she sees it and asks about it. Then answer, romantically, "I'm overwhelmed."

2. Allow your worrying to make you paranoid, causing you to stare intently at her as much as possible. This creates a sense of intimacy.

3. Permit your insecurity to slow you down. Slowing down, hesitating, pausing, and withholding are tantalizing.

4. Yield to your nervousness about her response until you are exquisitely attuned to the things she says. Listen for them and do things that prompt (from her) expressions of pleasure.

5. Let your anxiety about your performance prevent you from asking, "Was I good?" or "Am I the best?" Keep those questions to yourself. Worry about whether you would still be good, or the best, if you demanded praise.

The Anxious Female Lover

1. Let your anxiety make you giddy, flushed, and a little wild and uncontrolled. That's sexy.

2. If you feel any insecurity about your body, use it. Let it make you coquettish. Hesitate while disrobing. Reveal little flashes here, conceal little parts there. A certain reticence about revealing all is seductive, as strippers and veil dancers have proven for centuries.

3. Worry that he might have all the fun. To be sure you get yours, give him some direction. Make your preferences known.

4. Worry that, no matter how intimate you are physically, you're not getting to know each other in other ways. Talk, make contact, tell jokes.

5. Permit your anxiety to make you afraid to ask, afterward, about what he thinks of the state of the relationship. Heed your worry. Don't ask.

Worried to Distraction

One aspect of sex in which worrying can play an especially positive role is that of climax prevention.

The things men force themselves to think about in order to stave off orgasm (and, thus, to better satisfy their partners) are well known. They include song lyrics, mental replays of favorite sporting events, state capitals, speeches from Shakespeare, and puzzles ("Name three movies with titles that start with the letter *L*.") And yet such tricks and ploys are often only marginally successful, because they restrict their activity to the intellectual sphere.

Abstract cogitation is all well and good, but to really shift attention from the many pleasures and stimuli of actual sex, what's required is a distraction on the emotional level. That's where worrying can help.

Worrying is intense mental concentration with extreme emotional engagement. The more worried you are, the less you can think about, feel, or even notice anything else. This makes worrying, for men, the ideal strategy for taking their minds off the one thing they think about all the rest of the time except now, when they actually get a chance to do it—sex.

This, then, is worrying at its finest and most pure: the more worried you become, the more you're distracted from the task at hand, and the greater the payoff.

Worry Your Way to Climax-Delay

Forget the words to "I've Got a Little List" or the play-by-play of that 1989 Phillies-Astros playoff game. Instead, concentrate fully on the topics listed below, and be sure to fully embrace the scariness of their implications.

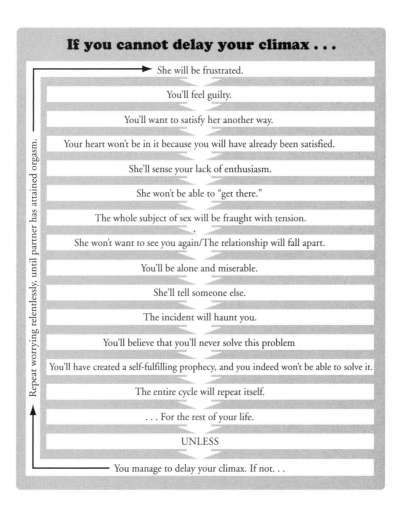

If you cannot delay your climax . . .

She will be frustrated.

You'll feel guilty.

You'll want to satisfy her another way.

Your heart won't be in it because you will have already been satisfied.

She'll sense your lack of enthusiasm.

She won't be able to "get there."

The whole subject of sex will be fraught with tension.

She won't want to see you again/The relationship will fall apart.

You'll be alone and miserable.

She'll tell someone else.

The incident will haunt you.

You'll believe that you'll never solve this problem

You'll have created a self-fulfilling prophecy, and you indeed won't be able to solve it.

The entire cycle will repeat itself.

. . . For the rest of your life.

UNLESS

You manage to delay your climax. If not. . .

Repeat worrying relentlessly, until partner has attained orgasm.

How She Can Help Defer His Climax

By occasionally murmuring something appropriately worrisome and distracting to her lover, a woman can help give him pause and delay his sexual culmination, but not frighten him so much that he flees in panic into the night.

The bar graph shows the delaying effects of various topics, when whispered to the male partner.

Comparative Climax-Delaying Efficacy of Worry Topics

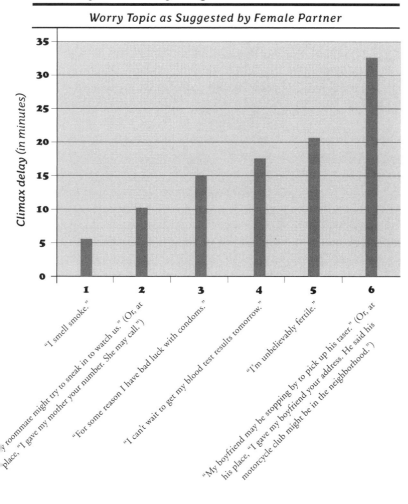

Worry Topic as Suggested by Female Partner

Climax delay (in minutes)

1 — "I smell smoke."

2 — "...y roommate might try to sneak in to watch us." (Or, at ...place, "I gave my mother your number. She may call.")

3 — "For some reason I have bad luck with condoms."

4 — "I can't wait to get my blood test results tomorrow."

5 — "I'm unbelievably fertile."

6 — "My boyfriend may be stopping by to pick up his taser." (Or, at his place, "I gave my boyfriend your address. He said his motorcycle club might be in the neighborhood.")

We are up too high. What if we fall? Oh, my God... I have to get off this cake right now...
What's in this cake? Sugar? Wheat?? EGGS???

LOVE AND MARRIAGE

Worry Your Way from Bedding to Wedding

Many people newly in love spend much of their time wondering "Am I in love?" much as a confused and weary business traveler will look around at a vaguely familiar airport and wonder "Am I in Indianapolis?" This fascinating state, known as "not knowing whether or not you're in love," is often accompanied by a feeling of foolishness, since it would seem one of the easiest things in the world to know whether or not you're possessed by this world-famous emotion.

But in fact it's not so easy. There are a number of quasi- and pseudo-love emotions that mimic or simulate being in love without actually being it: Infatuation. Really liking. Having a crush on. Finding yourself getting involved with. Having the hots for. Being obsessed with. Loving but not—you know—*in love with*.

How can you tell what it is you're feeling?

One good way is to examine the things you're worried about.

Is It Love

If you're worried...	it's really...
about where he/she is, what he/she is thinking, who he/she is seeing, and what he/she is doing all the time . . .	TRUE LOVE.
because he/she said he/she would call at 1:00 and it's now 1:10 . . .	*LOVE-BUT-NOT-LOVE.*
because he/she is talking to someone who isn't you . . .	OBSESSIVE SICKO LOVE.
because he/she isn't flirting back or isn't really sincere . . .	A CRUSH.
because you wonder whether he/she loves you and sort of hope he/she doesn't, really . . .	INFATUATION.
about whether he/she's worried about anything, and about whether he/she knows how you feel . . .	LUST.

What? Us Worry? The Follies of Love

"Yes," someone will say. "But when you're in love, you're really not worried about anything!"

Wrong. This widely held belief, which is reinforced by a million simpleminded pop songs, is utterly untrue. In fact, people who fall in love enter a new and exciting realm of worrying. *Worry* is the source of the energy that makes lovers feel so alive. *Worry* is what generates the vitality and world-embracing optimism that people in love so gladly and openly display. When you're in love, you have so much—which means you have so much more to worry about. It's worry that courses through your veins, more powerful than adrenaline.

For example: When you're in love, you're worried about whether or not your beloved returns your affections. Does she love me? Does she love me as much as I love her? Will she still love me tomorrow?

Or say she does love you. Then other worries arise: Does she love me more than I love her? Will I still love *her* tomorrow?

Or say you're convinced you love each other the same amount. Do your worries end there? Of course not: Should we get married? But I loved my first wife, and look how that turned out. Is this different? Is it different from her first marriage? And what about children?

Love is not the end of worry. As the song says, "We've only just begun . . . "

Try, Try Again: Worry Her into Loving You

Worrying about unrequited love, or insufficiently reciprocated love, can make us feel empty, miserable, and frustrated.

And that's terrific!

Because where there is worry, there is hope. When your feelings of love aren't reciprocated, it seems like all is lost. But all is not lost. It's just misplaced. And it can be found—in worrying itself.

If you play your cards right, you can use worry to win the heart of your beloved. This requires a special seven-step approach.

The Seven-Step Plan to Worrying Your Way to Romantic Success

1. *Be publicly unworried about yourself.* Let one and all see you being vibrant and upbeat.

2. *Worry to your beloved's friends about others' concern for him or her.* Worry to your beloved's friends about the things other

friends and colleagues have said about him or her around the office or at the gym. When they ask what you mean, apologize and mutter that you knew you shouldn't have said anything.

3. *Worry to your beloved's best friend about your concern for him or her.* Spy on your beloved during his or her daily routine — visits to the dry cleaner's, vegetable stands, and so on. Then tell his or her best friend that you think your beloved "seems distracted." Say that you encountered him or her on the street, citing the specific day and time, and that you said hello but he or she seemed not to recognize you. Reluctantly admit that you're worried.

4. *Emotionally outflank your beloved.* When you run into your beloved, treat him or her like an old lover you're glad to see after all these years and act as if you assume he or she feels the same way. Tell the beloved that you're glad to hear he or she is seeing someone, because you were a little worried that he or she would end up alone. Say, with unconvincing enthusiasm, "I mean, at least you've found *someone.*" Then leave.

5. *Plant your worry in your beloved.* Spy on him or her. When you see him or her coming out of a shop, rush up, panting, and say, "Sorry I'm late, I got held up." When he or she says he or she doesn't know what the hell you're talking about, get angry. Say, "This was your idea. Call me when you want to talk." Leave in a huff.

6. *Induce worry in your beloved that only you can assuage.* Arrange to have a drink with your beloved to hash things out "once and for all," and bring one of your friends (of the same sex as your beloved) to the rendezvous. Don't explain why your friend is there; instead, introduce your friend and then (affectionately)

ask him or her to leave you and your beloved for a while. Once alone, express worry to your beloved over his or her recent behavior. Say that you understand that your beloved's life "hasn't turned out the way you expected it would." (Whose has?) Ask what you can do to help, "not as a friend, but as someone who used to be in love with you." As soon as your beloved starts to answer, look at your watch, say you have to catch up with your friend, and add, "Look, I know you're worried. It's OK. Call me." Smile pityingly, leave money for the drinks, and exit.

7. Go home and wait for the phone to ring.

Tying the Slipknot: The Longevity of Marriage

We know, from reports in the media, from the divorces of those around us, and especially from our own divorces, that marriages usually start out with the most sincere of intentions but can founder on the rocks of almost anything.

But we have not been able to anticipate (and, thus, prepare for) when a given marriage will fail—until now. Through advances in the study of statistics and worry dynamics, it is now possible to know, based on objective, quantifiable data, how long we can expect any given marriage to last.

Although a marriage is a relationship, a subjective state of emotional being, we are now able to obtain objective, standardized measurements of a marriage by analyzing what the couple worries about. Once we quantify that, we have a decent chance of predicting the union's longevity.

Marriage Longevity Calculator

A. In the table below, circle the number that most closely reflects how much you and your partner worry about the following topics, from 0 ("Never") to 3 ("Endlessly") for each Worry Topic listed. Enter a value on which both spouses are in substantial agreement. Cheating, inflating or deflating the actual values, or otherwise skewing the real number will subvert the efficacy of the formula and become just one more example of the fact that your marriage is a sham and the two of you are living a lie.

The Longevity Calculator

Worry Topic	Never	A bit	A lot	Endlessly
1. Money	0	1	2	3
2. House and home	0	1	2	3
3. Sex	0	1	2	3
4. Your in-laws and relatives	0	1	2	3
5. Household chores	0	1	2	3
6. How you support and/or subvert each other in public	0	1	2	3
7. Neighbors	0	1	2	3
8. Kids	0	1	2	3
9. Career(s)	0	1	2	3
10. Politics and world events	0	1	2	3

Add up the total number of Worry Points (W) _____ .

B. Fill in the following biographical information:

(Y) We have been married ————— years.

(K) We have ————— children.

(N) This is the ————— (1st, 2nd, etc.) marriage for one of us, and the ————— marriage for the other, for a total of ————— .

C. Using the values above, solve the equation, below, where X = Predicted Longevity of Marriage in Years.

$$X = \frac{(Y \times 30)}{(W + 1)} \times \frac{(K + 1)}{N}$$

Example I
Bob and Sue have been married for four years. They have 10 Worry Points. They have one child. This is Bob's second marriage and Sue's first. Thus:

W = 10
Y = 4
K = 1
N = 2 + 1 = 3

$$X = \frac{(Y \times 30)}{(W + 1)} \times \frac{(K + 1)}{N}$$

or:

$$X = \frac{(4 \times 30)}{(10 + 1)} \times \frac{(1 + 1)}{3} = \frac{120}{11} \times \frac{2}{3} = \frac{240}{33} = 7.27$$

So, Bob and Sue can expect their marriage to last another 7.27 years. The benefits of knowing this number are substantial:

- Both partners may be less tempted to engage in affairs or flings, knowing they only have about seven years and three months left before the marriage will end and they will be single again.

- Both partners may also be more tempted to engage in affairs or flings, believing that, since the marriage is destined to end, it can't do that much harm.

- The primary wage earner can start saving money for spousal and child support now, rather than squander it today on SUVs and trips to Antigua, only to have to scramble for cash once the divorce is final.

- Each parent can make it his or her business to be especially loving, understanding, and supportive toward their child, laying solid groundwork for the post-divorce jockeying for the kid's affections. The child, of course, is the main beneficiary of this, which is as it should be.

- Fights and resentments over what to purchase—plasma TV or new kitchen cabinets; cable modem service or health club membership—become a thing of the past. Why make a fuss when you know that in seven years you'll be out of there?

Example2

Tony and Gail have been married one year. They circled 3 ("Endlessly") for all ten Worry Topics. They have no children. This is the first marriage for each of them. Thus, their calculation runs as follows:

W = 30
Y = 1
K = 0
N = 1 + 1 = 2

$$X = \frac{(1 \times 30)}{(30 + 1)} \; x \; \frac{(0 + 1)}{2} = \frac{30}{31} \; x \; \frac{1}{2} = \frac{30}{62} = 0.4838$$

Thus, their marriage will last for about another six months. Here's how Tony and Gail stand to benefit from this knowledge:

- Either or both might think, "Why wait?" and end the relationship now, before rancor sets in, while they still love each other.

- It is likely that they would take special care to avoid having children, thus sparing the baby the trauma, confusion, and weirdness of enduring a divorce four months before he or she is born.

- Any magazine subscriptions, NPR memberships, or joint club memberships destined to expire within that six-month period can be safely allowed to lapse, pending a new address for one or both partners.

- Important benchmarks—birthdays of the spouse, anniversaries, and other events—that will occur more than six months from now can be forgotten, without guilt.

• Special plans that have particular meaning to the couple—travel to certain places, visits to certain restaurants—can be accelerated, to be realized "before it's too late," sparing the partners later regret that they missed important opportunities while they were together.

Example3

Jean and Phil have been married for seven years. They have five children. Since they circled 0 ("Never") for all ten Worry Topics, they have no worries at all. (This is hypothetical, remember.) This is the first marriage for each of them.

W = 0
Y = 7
K = 5
N = 1 + 1 = 2

$$X = \frac{(7 \times 30)}{(0 + 1)} \times \frac{(5 + 1)}{2} = \frac{210}{1} \times \frac{6}{2} = \frac{1260}{2} = 630$$

That is, they can expect to be married for another 630 years, supported by their many happy children.

Your Longevity Calculations

PREGNANCY

When and Why to Worry with One on the Way

Congratulations! You're pregnant!

Pregnancy provides very fertile ground for worrying. Indeed, few people have as much access to worry as a pregnant woman, especially in the case of her first child. Not only does she get to worry about the usual things she's been worrying about all her life—her diet, her health, her marriage (or lack thereof), her finances—but she also gets to worry about all sorts of issues on behalf of the baby. That means fretting about the same problems from two perspectives—twice as much anxiety in the same amount of time, because now she's worrying for two!

Additionally, she worries across all dimensions of the space-time continuum. While most people worry about the present and the future, the expectant mom also gets to worry about the past. For example, anyone at a cocktail party can worry about whether she should have another martini. But a woman who has just discovered she is pregnant finds herself worrying about the martinis she drank *last month*, and what effect they might have on the baby.

No wonder women the world over greet the news of their pregnancy with such excitement. No wonder they exhibit that famous glow. They have entered a period in their lives in which they are free to worry about absolutely everything, twice as hard, all the livelong day.

Housecleaning Through Hand-Wringing

One of the drearier realities of being pregnant is that the normal, day-to-day concerns of life that beset the nonpregnant person don't go away. No matter how far along you are, you still have to do the things you did before you became pregnant.

Among these tasks is cleaning the house or apartment. A woman in the final weeks of pregnancy may have a valid excuse (or even a doctor's note) for not dusting, vacuuming, or clearing away clutter. But until then, even a mom-to-be with a hired cleaning person has chores aplenty. But they're just too tedious and exhausting to even think about. What to do?

The answer is simple: Fear the worst. Focus on all the bad things that might happen if you *don't* clean. In a word, worry, and watch your motivation for cleaning skyrocket.

Cleanup Motivation: Worry as Dustbuster

Don't kid yourself. Dust isn't some sort of harmless indoor snow. It consists mainly of dead skin cells and dust mites, which under a microscope look like horrifying monsters. Are you really willing to let your fragile baby breathe all this in, or absorb it, *in utero*, through you? Get the dust rag and the spray and get busy!

If you need more motivation, worry about how, ever since you became pregnant, you haven't gotten enough exercise. Grab that vacuum cleaner and pretend it's either a jet ski (for uprights) or a hockey stick (for canisters), turn it on, and zoom or skate your way to robust health and clean floors.

Little Big Mom: Throwing Your Weight Around at Work

Pregnant women are both feared and revered by men, especially in the workplace. Even the most enlightened male views pregnancy as a sort of trans-human paranormal state in which the woman receives special spiritual powers, suffers psychological and intellectual handicaps, and metamorphoses into something both much more and much less than a normal, competent person.

This can make it especially hard for you to do your job. Men who act like garden-variety sexist jerks around nonpregnant women become Ultra Jerks when a colleague is with child. How can you cope with the patronizing praise and condescending dismissal of men who think your enlarging tummy means a shrinking brain?

It's easy, and it's fun. And it allows you to take advantage of the worrying you're already doing, for example, the fear that you're too big and bloated and are doomed to remain a waddling, lactating blimp forever.

Forget trying to pretend that you're not gigantic, heavy, or graceless. Instead, welcome your worry. *Embrace* your fear of blimpiness. *Feel* your big fat tubby clumsiness. Then visualize mammoth, powerful figures from movies and adopt their majesty, their authority, and their scary bigness as your own (see chart, "Think Big," page 98). Shift slowly in your chair, make vaguely exhausted gestures, sigh wearily. Speak as they speak, or as they would speak if they could. Then stand back and wait for the results!

Welcome Wisdom from Within

Many people treat a pregnant woman as though she were public property, a cross between a statue in the park and a candidate running for office. Strangers think nothing of asking if they can touch your tummy, while friends just go ahead and touch. Women, and some men, passing you in a store or a restaurant offer unsolicited advice. Your mother, your partner's mother, your friends' mothers—everyone has an opinion, and so do their sisters and their cousins and their aunts.

They act this way because they're worried, both for you and your baby. Isn't that wonderful? And yet, especially if you're a first-time

Think Big

Problem at Work	Visualise...	and say:
You are ignored in a meeting.	Jabba the Hutt	"Kindly do not make me have to raise my voice."
Man dismisses your idea.	Marlon Brando as Don Corleone	"I don't understand. I try to treat you with respect and this is how you repay me?"
Woman dismisses your idea.	King Kong	"You. Be quiet. I have a good idea. You will listen."
Adversary doesn't take you seriously.	Sidney Greenstreet in *The Maltese Falcon*	"By God, but you amuse me, you certainly do. I like a man/woman who likes a woman who is with child and attempts to ease her burden by ignoring her completely. But such gestures of thoughtful accommodation are entirely unnecessary in my case, I assure you."

mom for whom every day of pregnancy is a new experience, chances are you respond to their worry not with reassurance but with worry of your own. What if they're right? What if they're privy to some pregnancy folk-wisdom of which you, and your fancy-schmancy OB-GYN, are oblivious? What if you're doing something wrong?

Actually, unless you're smoking crack and jumping nightly on a trampoline, you're probably fine. But that doesn't mean you can't use their worry and your worry to your own advantage.

First, whenever any of these helpful experts suggests that you're doing the wrong thing (or not doing the right thing), take their condemnations to heart and worry. *Hard.* Exaggerate its effects. If possible, grow pale. Let your breathing change, your eyes get glassy, and so on. Then look off into the middle distance as though listening to a voice from deep inside, as if you're receiving a communication from the womb.

Then whip out any one of the small, portable, increasingly incomprehensible devices being produced by the computer and entertainment and telecommunications industries, and pretend to use it to *consult the fetus* and get its response to this latest bit of advice or criticism. Tell your advisors what the baby has "told" you. Look even more worried, and see what you can extort out of them and their concern.

Who's to say that such a feat isn't possible? Who can keep up with all the things a cell phone, let alone the more esoteric digital gizmos, can do nowadays? There are many props on the market, both at stores and on-line. Simply select which props appeal to you, learn your cues, and rehearse some basic lines. But don't forget to worry, because that's what will sell the scene.

Baby "Talk"

Deal with unsolicited advice by "consulting" the fetus.

Where: On street
What Unsolicited Advisor Says: "You really shouldn't be out in this weather, you know, dear."
Prop: Stethoscope
Action: Place ear pieces in ears and touch 'scope to tummy. Move slowly, listening.
You Say: "Oh, no—now you've made the baby upset. She's worried that she might catch a cold, and she wants to know if you'll lend us your scarf."

Where: Coffee shop, café, other lunch place
What Unsolicited Advisor Says: "Coffee? You're ordering coffee? I never drank coffee when I was expecting."
Prop: Mobile phone
Action: Take out phone, and touch several buttons. Hold phone to tummy, then put phone to ear. Say, "Are you sure?" Hold phone to tummy, then put to ear again and listen.
You Say: "The baby says that the reason we drink coffee is that I'm so tired all the time. He wonders if you wouldn't mind doing our grocery shopping tomorrow."

Where: Nice restaurant
What Unsolicited Advisor Says: "Excuse me, but how can you drink wine when you're pregnant? I never heard of such a thing."
Prop: MP3 player, GPS unit, other small device

Action: Touch device to tummy, hold for a moment. Press any button on device, then hold to your ear.

You Say: "You've gotten the baby extremely upset. I'll have to take her home now and eat oatmeal and drink warm milk. This meal has been completely ruined, and I think you should pay the check."

Where: Gym

What Unsolicited Advisor Says: "Are you sure you should be working out like this? In your condition?"

Prop: Headphones

Action: Wear headphones with wire disappearing under clothes. Hold up your hand for quiet and listen intently.

You Say: "The baby says he's going to run me ragged once he's born, so I'd better get into shape now, however I can. But it would help if you came over and washed my windows."

For Men Only: Follow Your Blocker

You may not be the pregnant one, but that doesn't mean you don't get to share in the thrills and benefits and joys of worrying. There are big advantages to be derived by parlaying your own worry and the worry of others. Who are these "others"?

Other men.

Practically all men find the presence of a pregnant woman unsettling and worrisome. For men, pregnancy is perhaps the most alien experience imaginable, even more Wholly Other than menstrual cramps or pedicures. Men don't know for sure how fragile a pregnant woman is. They don't know how much to defer to her. They don't know what the etiquette is, they don't know what they're supposed to do—in sum, they just don't know anything.

Assertive Pregnancy Worry

You want...	You say...
A CAB THAT HAS STOPPED FOR SOMEONE ELSE ON A RAINY NIGHT.	"I've got a pregnant woman here. She must get out of the rain at once!"
A TABLE AT A CROWDED RESTAURANT.	"We need to get this woman in and out of the restaurant as soon as possible. And we need a quiet table, with lots of space."
"FRONTSIES" IN A LONG LINE AT AIRPORT CHECK-IN.	"Excuse us, we have a delicate medical condition here. We must get through and get seated as soon as possible."
PREFERENTIAL TREATMENT ALMOST ANYWHERE.	"I beg your pardon. This woman is pregnant. Please show her some courtesy."

As the partner and companion of a pregnant woman, you can take advantage of other men's discomfiture by practicing Assertive Pregnancy Worry so you can cash in big at restaurants, banks, and other public places.

Think about football. Recall how great runners know how to follow—and direct—their blockers, especially during kickoffs and punt returns. That's what you can do with your pregnant woman, albeit figuratively. Employ her as a wedge, allowing you to cut into long lines, gain preferential treatment, and indulge in selfish behavior. To do this you'll need to understand what worries you about her pregnancy, and then aim at those fears in others, especially men.

Getting in Shape for the Little One

By building up the worry muscles now, during pregnancy, parents and caregivers can prepare themselves for the demands of worried parenthood. As in any training for an arduous activity, the essential elements are patience, steady application, and a willingness to challenge oneself enough, but not too much.

Follow the training program in the table on pages 104–105. Remember to warm up before each session and to cool down afterward.

Worry about the suggested issues in order, for the specified length of time. Preface all Worry Issues with spoken or unspoken "What if I . . . ?"

Bear in mind that the topics you're worrying about are not those that will concern you as a parent. "What if my water breaks and I don't know it?" will not be an issue once the baby arrives. Rather, you are using anxiety about pregnancy to get in shape for the Olympic-class challenge of later parental worrying. In these exercises, don't worry about what you're worrying about. Just worry about your worrying.

Worry Training

Situation	Issue (Time)
	WARMUP
BABY SHOWER	What if I . . . ? • don't know whether to invite X, who's having fertility problems (1:20) • don't like most gifts (1:00) • get same diaper bag from three people (1:00) • am offended by Jane, mother of three, and her jokes about how I'm too "lazy" and "self-centered" to be a good mother (1:25)
PLANNING TO NAME THE BABY	What if I . . . ? • can't think of a good name (1:30) • don't want to offend relatives (1:30) • can't find a name book that isn't stupid (1:35) • think baby doesn't "look like" any one name (1:40)
	FIRST ROUTINE
CHOOSING DELIVERY METHOD	What if I . . . ? • don't trust my husband to be a good enough Lamaze coach (2:00) • choose home birthing and end up needing hospital care (2:15) • choose home birthing and end up needing a whole new sofa (2:20) • don't like my midwife (2:25) • realize my midwife doesn't like me (2:30) • can't get to the hospital in time (2:40) • can't say "doula" without laughing (2:45)

Situation	Issue (Time)
	SECOND ROUTINE
LABOR AND DELIVERY	What if I . . . ? • chicken out and demand drugs right after signing hospital admission form (2:50) • say horrible things to husband/Lamaze coach (3:00) • say horrible things to doctors, who refuse to give me drugs (3:00) • think husband is flirting with nurse (3:20) • scream, shriek, and act like Linda Blair in *The Exorcist* (3:30) • end up hating baby because of pain (3:45) • end up hating husband because of pain (3:45) • end up liking pain (4:00)
	COOL-DOWN
POST-NATAL RECOVERY	What if I . . . ? • think baby is ugly (4:00) • don't bond with baby (3:50) • bond with baby but don't bond with husband (3:30) • allow myself to be bullied by maternity-ward nurses (3:00) • don't like breastfeeding (2:40) • want to breastfeed baby for next eight years (2:30) • feel like I'll never want to have sex again (2:15) • never have sex again (2:00) • feel like I don't know how to be a mother (1:45) • realize this was how my mother felt (1:30) • realize my mother was right (1:00) • don't know what to do next (0:30)

PARENTING

The Worry Years

Parenting and worrying: Is there any difference between the two? Actually, yes. The job of parenting changes and even diminishes as the child becomes an adult. Worrying is eternal and unchanging.

But the symbiotic, if not synonymous, relationship between parenting and worrying is captured in the following true anecdote: A young woman of high-school age was out late one evening— so late that her parents went to bed before she had returned home. Her father fell into an untroubled slumber, but her mother sat up, fretting and brooding and imagining a variety of disasters that might have befallen their daughter. Finally the mother could stand it no longer. She looked down, punched her husband, and said, "Wake up. It's your turn to worry," at which point the man took over worrying and the woman went to sleep.

Parents are experts at worrying, just as fish are experts at swimming. Still, even experts can use a few tips now and then, particularly if they want to derive more joy from their worrying. Readers who are not yet parents may want to review what follows, either as a form of birth control, or in preparation for the occurrence, one day, of the blessed event.

As for kids, they'll learn in these pages just how worried their folks are, or could be. This is an enormously useful insight. It shows just how much parents are, in the end, human beings. And it shows how they can be manipulated.

Signs of Worry

Remember those yellow "Baby on Board" signs? Remember how they were suction-cupped to the windows of Volvos and Hondas everywhere, announcing that it would be especially terrible and heinous to smash into the car in question because, its worthless adult passengers aside, this car held an actual baby? Did it really inspire other people to drive more safely?

It doesn't matter. The purpose of such signs isn't to ask (or demand) that the world show your little one special deference. The sign is placed there by the parent as a testament to his or her worrying, to be read and appreciated by the parents themselves.

And why not? Worrying about your baby is perhaps the most admirable, blameless, unsullied, pure, noble, and praiseworthy thing you can do in American society. But why stop with "Baby on Board"?

Flaunt your parental concern with an entire series of specific signs. Your baby will get nurturing, one-on-one socializing interactivity with strangers, you'll win admiring looks from one and all, and you'll both share the joy of knowing that, when it comes to a display of lovingly obsessive worry over every aspect of your child's existence, you're well and truly "on board."

Here are other signs of worrying, caring, and love, to be affixed in the appropriate place:

For Parents of Babies and Toddlers:
What We Worry About When We Worry

When we worry about young children, we worry about things that haven't happened yet—which is of course the nature of all worry. But, significantly, we worry about a person *to whom very little has ever happened at all.* How, then, do we know what to worry about? The list of potential disasters, mishaps, tragedies, and problems is infinite. And yet obviously we don't worry about every conceivable possibility. We select.

One mother worries about her son eating poison, but another doesn't. One father takes brisk steps to prevent his daughter from sticking her finger into an electrical outlet, but another deals with it in a more leisurely fashion or not at all.

Why? How do we know what problems are more likely to befall an individual whose personal history offers so few precedents for study?

We don't. We project our inner fears and worries onto our kids. We don't worry *for them* because of who they are; we worry *at them* because of who *we* are. But suppose we are worried about the wrong things? This is a wonderful worry for parents, for it can lead to

Self-Help Worrying About Children

If you're worried about your child...	you do this for the child:	And you can do this for yourself:
catching a cold . . .	dress child warmly.	buy yourself new, warm clothes; take vacation to a warm climate.
being water safe . . .	enroll child in swim lessons.	join a swim club; buy a boat.
being safe in the car . . .	get latest, most expensive car seat and never let child ride in front.	buy luxury car that is bigger and heavier; buy two-seat roadster so child can never ride in it at all.
banging head on corners of tables . . .	temporarily pad your furniture; give child a helmet.	replace all furniture with new furniture.
not getting enough sleep . . .	put the child to bed early.	have your friends over for a party.

more and more worry. And the rewards for this kind of escalating worry are considerable. The world gives us total credit for being selfless, for putting this little person's needs above our own. Indeed, we give ourselves credit for it, too. It's one of the most beautiful and joyful aspects of being a parent, and of being a worrier.

In practice, parents can effectively indulge themselves and reap enormous personal gain by boot-strapping their (unexpressed) desires onto their worries about their children, and then fretting accordingly.

Share the Worry, Share the Joy

Some of the most satisfying moments in a parent's life are those spent teaching, pursuing activities or projects with the child in an effort both to impart explicit knowledge and to convey, by example, particular attitudes and values. This applies to everything from riding a bike to cheering for a team to loving your partner.

And, of course, to worrying. A child's initiation into the world of worrying is one of the most cherished rites of passage in life. By encouraging every twinge of anxiety, by fanning each tiny spark of fear, the parent helps mold and nurture the child's developing self.

The parent also gets to relive the experience of his first worry by seeing it through the bright, shining, troubled eyes of his offspring.

Some of a kid's ability to worry is inherent and unchangeable; it's part of the child's *nature*. But the ability to worry can also be acquired and developed with exposure and experience, through *nurturing*.

As with any valuable activity, worrying and its essential techniques should be taught from an early age. Any activity will do: throwing a ball, making a sandwich, feeding the ducks at the park. It hardly matters what you do, as long as you do it, worriedly, together. When a parent teaches a child to worry, qualm time is quality time.

Suggested Activities for Parent-Child Fun and Fretting

- **Play Catch.** Watch your child miss the simplest lobs and throw feebly and wildly in all directions. **You'll worry** that his complete lack of athletic skills will sabotage his life forever. **Your child will worry**, when he sees you looking concerned and disappointed, that you don't love him because he's not any good at it. You'll both **share the joy** of having a challenge to work on.

- **Go on a Picnic.** Pack sandwiches, chips, drinks, and napkins, and spread out a blanket in the park, at the beach, or just in the backyard. **You'll worry** that bugs, dirt, and bad weather will somehow ruin everything. Because of that, **your child will worry** that the natural world is a dangerous, hostile place. For the rest of your lives you'll **share the joy** of having a common enemy, nature.

- **Go to a Baseball Game.** Box seats, upper deck, bleachers— it doesn't matter, as long as you're together. **You'll worry** that your child's wandering attention and increasing boredom means that her IQ isn't what you had hoped, or she's not the athletic, spunky, ball-playing kid you were. **Your child will worry** that, because you've forced her to sit for three hours watching something she doesn't care about and can't understand, surrounded by noisy, scary strangers, she's being punished for some mysterious infraction you refuse to acknowledge. You'll **share the joy** and cheer enthusiastically when the game is over.

- **Make Cookies.** Great for a rainy afternoon. **You'll worry** that the flour strewn all over the kitchen will take forever to clean up, that the eggshells in the dough will add a disgusting crunch to the cookies, and that your child will want to taste the dough, which includes forbidden raw eggs. **Your child will worry** that cooking is stressful, he's no good at it anyway, and it's somehow wrong to want to taste things. You'll **share the joy** of laughing at how much the cookies resemble Sheetrock, and by the time you throw them away, the rain will have stopped.

• **Go to a Movie.** Hollywood has taken increased notice of the need for family films, and film companies are releasing more of them. **You'll worry** that you're paying a fortune for admission, sodas, and candy that will never separate from her teeth—all for a movie that will, soon and affordably, be out on video (and which you'll have to buy and watch endlessly). **Your child will worry**, as you brood, that you don't really want to see the movie, and she'll conclude that she'd really rather be seeing it with her friends. You'll **share the joy** of both having not enjoyed the movie, and having to pretend that you did. That's bonding!

For Parents of Teenagers: Your Declaration of Their Independence

The parents of teenagers experience the purest and most intense form of worrying known to science—and for good reason. It is the teenager's cultural and genetic job to cause parental worry in order to separate from the parent's control and, thus, to attain adulthood. As this process advances, the parent's concern increases just as the parent's ability to affect the teenager's behavior decreases.

The more the parent worries, the less the teenager listens. Crushed by the futility of it all, the parent tries to give up. But she can't give up. It's her child. So she resumes worrying.

This on-again, off-again alternating worry current is boosted by the many paradoxes of teenagehood. Teenagers are children who aren't children. Hormonally they're mature adults; emotionally they're spoiled brats. They insist you get completely out of their lives but somehow remain on call to provide money, transportation, and on-line access. They're able to do all the risky things adults do—drinking, driving, drinking and driving, having sex, getting pregnant, doing drugs, buying things, stealing things, breaking laws—but take little or no responsibility for the outcome of their behavior. And then of course they lie about it all.

Teenagers keep secrets about everything and then laugh when their parents don't know what they've been doing, or whom they've been doing it with, or at whose house they've been doing it when they said whose parents would be home when they really weren't. They share nothing, and then they get huffy and sulk because no one understands.

No wonder their parents worry. And that suits everyone—teens, parents, society, human evolution—just fine. The more a parent worries, the more alienated a teen becomes—and that promotes separation and adult independence. Indeed, *the more you worry, the better a parent you are.*

Sometimes, though, you listen to a teenager answer your question, and it seems that there really is nothing to worry about. Such statements as "I was researching a paper on the Internet" and "I'm meeting Emily at the mall" seem to be straightforward assertions with no secret, worriable content.

But don't be deceived. Even the most innocent-seeming teenage statement is chock-full of possibilities for worrying your teenager into a happy, healthy, independent, worried adulthood.

Teenspeak 101

You ask your son or daughter what's going on, and he or she offers a perfectly acceptable explanation. So there's nothing to worry about, right?

Of course not.

Below are some basic "innocent" teenage statements, together with their likely real meanings, all of which provide ample opportunities for fretting and incipient panic—and a great basis for getting to understand your teenager.

When He Says: "I'm hungry."
He Could Really Mean: "I'm stoned."

When He Says: "Nothing's the matter."
He Could Really Mean: "Everything's the matter."

When He Says: "Brianna is coming over to study."
He Could Really Mean: "We'll make out in the den but probably not really have sex, since you're home."

When She Says: "Jenna's family has two houses."
She Could Really Mean: "Jenna's family has a winter house and a summer house and we only have one. You're a failure."

When She Says: "I did my homework in study hall."
She Could Really Mean: "I'm blowing off homework, college, and the possibility of a career entirely."

When She Says: "Dirk's a drummer and I love him."
She Could Really Mean: "Dirk's a drummer and I love him."

10

AT HOME

The Place to Hang Your Worry

Every home, no matter how grand, modest, or god-awful, has chairs and sofas to sit on, tables to support things, lamps to dispel the darkness, and decorative objects to make the place look nice. Home is where you live with your spouse or companion, raise your children, care for your pets, entertain your friends, pursue your hobbies, cook and clean (assuming you ever actually do cook and clean), and take care of yourself in body, mind, and soul.

Any one of these aspects of domestic life can provide enough joyful worry opportunities to last a lifetime. Put them all together, and you really have to wonder why anyone ever leaves the house at all. There's so much at home to worry about!

Even the most humble snack table can, under the right circumstances, lead to accident, injury, or death. The emergency rooms of America (and the world!) fill up every day with people who have practically killed themselves installing a storm window or peeling a cucumber. And yet these dangers are especially hard to see. Why? Because they're in our home, where we've encountered these objects a thousand times and where we assume we are safe.

Danger-Proof Your Home the Worried Way

No matter how seemingly benign, almost every element of interior decoration can—and should—be worried about. Some pose immediate threats; others, more unlikely or completely impossible threats. The type of threats doesn't matter. By worrying about any and all of them, you'll find a variety of unexpected, hidden benefits.

Design element: **LAMPS**

WORRY: Bulbs can shatter; hot bulbs can burn hands; glowing filament can overheat room; power cords can trip guests, snarl vacuum cleaners, and annoy pets.

SOLUTION: Flashlights in every room

BENEFITS: Hand-held "task lighting" is extra-efficient; all rooms are bathed in romantic atmosphere; blown fuses, blackouts, and intruders are no problem, as flashlight is always ready at hand.

Design element: High-style **COFFEE TABLE**

WORRY: Low-rise table, in middle of room, can bang shins; hard to move to unfold sofa bed; difficult to vacuum under, therefore fosters unhealthful dirt

SOLUTION: Replace with surfboard on floor

BENEFITS: Waterproof; spills easily cleaned up; easy to move aside and replace; no banged shins; variety of styles and colors

Design element: **SOFA**

WORRY: Too-soft cushions can be difficult to get up out of, leading to back strain and embarrassment; coins, popcorn pieces, assorted junk collect under cushions and inside seams; impossible to vacuum underneath

SOLUTION: Gym-style bleachers

BENEFITS: Makes cleaning easy; provides arena seating for group TV watching, living room skits, large parties

Design element: Display of **OBJETS D'ART, TCHOTCHKES**
> WORRY: Can gather unhealthful dust; are easily knocked off shelves, broken; are easily stolen; waste shelf space; create feeling of clutter
> SOLUTION: Display in aquariums
> BENEFITS: More interesting than fish and don't have to be fed; water in tanks prevents dust buildup, theft, knocking over, and breakage

Design element: **AREA RUGS**
> WORRY: Skidding on loose rug can cause injuries; wrinkles, folds can cause tripping, sprained ankles
> SOLUTION: Paint rug pattern onto floor
> BENEFITS: Avant-garde design statement; easy to vacuum

Design element: **WALLS**
> WORRY: Too hard, can injure people who fall against them; need to be painted; holes from picture hanging need to be patched
> SOLUTION: Velcro floor rugs to walls
> BENEFITS: Safety, insulation from cold; quieter rooms; attractive wall coverings

Yesterday's Worries, Today's Hobbies

The home is a place of leisure, and fun, and hobbies—pastimes created for the express purpose of helping us *forget* our worries. Yet, paradoxically, worrying has played a central role in their creation and development. Many of the most popular pastimes we enjoy at home today were created by our ancient forebears in response to their worrying about what they encountered.

The Origin of Contemporary Hobbies

Who They Were	What They Worried About	Modern Hobby They Bequeathed to Us
Homo erectus	Killing scary buffalo; recording visual experience	Paint-by-numbers
Pretentious cave men; early French	Starvation; boredom at mealtime	Gourmet cooking
Early agricultural societies	Starving to death	Gardening
Ancient Persians	Martial strategy; military preparedness	Chess
Early Hindus, Buddhists	Poverty; suffering; death; reality; everything	Yoga
Medieval aristocracy	Boredom	Bridge, canasta, gin rummy, hearts, poker, and other card games
Renaissance courtiers	Maintaining status amid palace intrigues	Tennis and, ultimately, Ping-Pong
Renaissance scholars	Preserving artifacts of civilization	Stamp, coin collecting
Baroque-era Europeans	Pleasing royalty; praising God	Piano lessons
Preindustrial Northern Europeans	Catching a chill	Knitting

Entertaining: Saint Worry

When it comes to entertaining, it's always the same: cocktail party, dinner party, birthday party, Superbowl party, Oscar party, Tupperware party, exorcism, seance, orgy, or *bris*—all the so-called experts start with a single piece of advice to the would-be host: "Relax. Entertaining should be as much fun for you as it is for your guests. Enjoy it!"

Nonsense. The essence of entertaining is serving others: you clean, primp, cook, serve, enthuse, appreciate, and clean up. You care about everyone except yourself. You attend to people's most trivial requests. If a guest muses out loud that she might like a glass of water, you leap up and get it. You act with perfect selflessness.

You become, in other words, a saint.

Why? Because of worry.

As a host you experience two basic categories of worrying. You worry about (a) whether your guests will like what you've provided, and (b) what they'll think of you as a host. These two kinds of worry—usually alternating but sometimes experienced simultaneously—spur the host to the kind of noble, generous, altruistic behavior he or she would otherwise find completely alien.

When it comes to entertaining, worrying makes us saintly, and the best host is a worried host.

Last-Minute Things to Worry About to Guarantee a Successful Party

1. **Drugs**—Who knows what your guests might be allergic to, or when they might get a headache? Stock your medicine cabinet with one of every kind of antihistamine, analgesic, anti-asthma inhaler, and placebo. (Tourniquet and de-fib paddles are optional.)

2. **Bedding**—For guests who can't or shouldn't drive or even attempt to leave under their own power. Insist that they stay overnight. (Plus they can help you clean up tomorrow.)

3. **Politics**—Hide copies of any left-wing or right-wing magazines, and anything in between. Insults, sneering, hurt feelings, and rage commonly result from spirited political discussions.

4. **Religion**—Hide copies of the Bible, the Torah, the Koran, and other religious texts. Insults, sneering, hurt feelings, and rage commonly result from spirited religious discussions.

5. **Ashtrays**—Some people (possibly you) may smoke, but others (possibly you) may object. Have some on hand but not in obvious places.

6. **Ice and lemons**—There are never enough. And they both keep.

7. **Chocolate**—Sooner or later, most people want some. You'll be amazed at how putting out a little bowl of Raisinettes will have people calling you a genius.

8. **Food and drink**—It's a Jewish tradition to have not enough liquor and too much food. It's a WASP tradition to have not enough food and too much liquor. Other groups' traditions fall somewhere in between. Whatever yours is, be sure to have too much of both food and liquor, unless you and your guests don't drink alcohol, in which case have no liquor at all.

9. **Departure**—Stockpile videos of your (or anyone's) wedding or vacation. When you think the party's winding down and it's time for everyone to go, bring them out. It's an effective ploy for driving away guests, who will worry about getting stuck in your home forever.

10. **Everything else**—When you've completed the preparations suggested in items 1 through 9, and your guests are about to arrive, ask yourself: What am I forgetting? This question is, of course, impossible to answer and a source of endless worry. Thinking about it will make you look pained, earnest, and solicitous, like a concerned—and saintly—host.

DRIVING

The Road Worrier

Driving and worrying were made for each other.

During most drives of any substantial length, there's almost nothing else to do *but* worry. You can listen to the radio, but worrying liberates you from having to search for decent programming. You can listen to books on tape, but worrying is about your own life, and not the made-up life of some pretend person. You can listen to a CD, but worrying frees you from having to deal with all that technology. And you can converse with whomever you're driving with, but all they'll really want to talk about is *their* worries.

When you're worrying about your own worries, you're the writer, the director, and the star. The story is enormously compelling—because it's your story. You create a program precisely tailored to your own interests and road-related fears, and you find it deeply moving and relevant. And you do it inside your own head.

So let's gas up, start worrying, and take it on the road!

Caution: Worry-Free Drivers

The most dangerous drivers on the road are those who *don't* worry. They come in essentially two groups:

- **The reckless, devil-may-care young people** who weave in and out of lanes, cruise past you (even while you yourself are speeding) at a supersonic clip, and charge off entrance ramps onto freeways as though seeking escape velocity. They fail to worry, not only about driving, but about life itself—theirs, yours, and other people's.

- **The distracted, dottering old people** in their dark amber wraparound sunglasses, who sit in contented placidity and tool along at exactly the speed limit, or less.

One group refuses to worry while driving because they've never worried about anything in their limited lifetime. The other fails to worry while driving, either because they've lived a lifetime of worrying about everything else, and it's enough already, or because they believe they're driving safely and don't have to worry.

In either case, the reader is advised to leave the not-worrying to these two constituencies. The rest of us have plenty of things to worry about, starting with the fact that we have to share the road with them.

Are You Defensive Enough?

"Drive defensively" is one of the main catchphrases of automotive safety. And it's good advice—especially if others are driving defensively, since their defensive moves with regard to you will be, by definition, unpredictable. Thus, their defensiveness increases your defensiveness in an unending cycle. It's like the noise level in a restaurant: the louder things get, the louder everyone has to be in order to be heard over the loudness, which makes things even louder.

All of which means that simply driving defensively isn't enough. Every freeway cowboy, sober commuter, and soccer mom out there is driving defensively.

What we must aspire to is to drive *paranoically*.

If "driving defensively" means driving worried, then we must take that worrying to a higher level and employ worry at its most uninhibited and unconstrained. A worried driver is a safe driver, and a more worried driver is an even safer driver.

Tips for Ultra-Defensive Driving

1. *When pulling into traffic from a driveway:* Worry that no one sees you. The other drivers are busy defending themselves against the cars already on the road. The last place they're going to look is at somebody's driveway, which they think of as a place for driving into, not out of.

2. *When merging onto a highway:* You're entering the right lane, where the scaredy-cats drive. Worry about them being spooked by the very appearance of your car. If you let them pass, they will slow down to let you enter anyway, and soon the traffic on the entire highway will be dangerously slow and snarled. So skip the whole thing: take back roads and enjoy the scenery.

3. *When driving in high-speed traffic:* Pass others guardedly. Be anxious that the driver you pass may take offense that your old car is zooming past his newer and cooler car, that someone who looks like you is passing someone who looks like him, or that somehow you are putting him down. Beware the crazy, competitive drivers who might suddenly speed up to challenge you. Better to ease up, allow more time for your trip, and don't pass anyone.

4. *When turning left across opposing traffic at a stop light:* Do not assume the first oncoming car will yield to you, even if they are signaling to turn left, too. Do you turn left in front

of them, or do you pass them and *then* turn? Or you can wait to turn until there are no more oncoming cars, but then worry about all the car horns from the line of cars behind you, also waiting to turn. Best to make only right turns.

5. *When behind a car that is inexplicably far behind the car in front of it:* Assume the worst and worry, not that the driver in front of you is being careful, but that he or she is petrified and has no idea how to drive on a highway. "One car length for every ten miles per hour" was abandoned decades ago. Floor it and get away from them ASAP.

6. *When driving behind or beside someone at the wheel, talking on a cell phone:* Worry isn't the word. Treat them as though they were carrying nitroglycerin. Most people can't drive very well using two hands and all their attention. Assume the talking driver has an even more diminished capacity that could get worse if they got in an argument, turned on the radio, or simply forgot they were driving. Get away.

7. *When driving into, around, or out of a big parking lot:* Worry about the fact that no one knows the rules of this weird, ambiguous zone. Plus, there are pedestrians, strollers, and bicycles. Avoid malls and big parking lots. Don't shop, and save money.

8. *When caught in a highway traffic jam:* Worry obsessively that, at random intervals, a maniac on a motorcycle will suddenly roar past you on either side, mere inches from your outside mirror. Because he will. Check rearview mirror often even though you're not moving.

9. *When driving on an icy or rain-slicked road:* If you have an antilock brake system (ABS), worry about what is controlling your car. You don't know what's going to happen when you step on the brakes. Should you pump, or will the brakes pump themselves—or, worse, stop working? In an emergency, you want to stop *fast,* not stop slower because the car might swerve; but with an ABS, you just don't know what the brakes are going to do. Try to avoid ABS. If your car has an ABS, avoid using the brakes.

10. *When tempted to assert your right-of-way:* If it comes down to a question of right-of-way, worry, not about what's legally yours, but about all the jerks out there who are unaware of it or who just don't care. Think of it not as a right but as a burden. Give it away.

Happy, Worried Motoring

But wait. Driving needn't be all fear, wariness, and pessimism. Worrying does keep us vigilant and thus helps us to stay alive. And that's important. But it's not the only benefit to be derived from worrying at the wheel. Driving can be fun, and worried driving can be even more fun, in a worried way.

Worrying Makes Driving Fun

1. **Worrying makes long trips pass more quickly.** Even when driving doesn't put you to sleep, it can be deeply boring and seem to go on and on. But not if you worry. A worried mind is an engaged mind, and an engaged mind makes the time fly.

2. **Worrying makes short trips more exciting.** Short car trips, through residential neighborhoods teeming with children, pets,

and cyclists, and through shopping districts crammed with traffic, demand more attention and faster reflexes. You must make more decisions, you encounter more distractions, and you're offered narrower margins for error. It's a blast!

3. **Worry turns parking into a James Bond–like experience.** The space might be too small, you might be taking too long and blocking traffic, you might bang into the car behind or in front, you might dent your car if you try to pull in headfirst—let your worries lead you to greatness. Slam through the gears, brake hard, jump out of the car with a macho "I'm-not-to-be-toyed-with" swinging shut of the door. You've not just parked; you've triumphed over the physical world. Walk away without looking back, using your keyless remote to lock the doors.

4. **Worry makes rush hour interesting.** Worry that you're in the slowest-moving lane, worry that someone is going to cut in front of you, worry that you're going to be late. Who says rush hour is boring? It's an action-adventure!

Keeping Kids Occupied and Worried

But what about the children?

Every parent knows that any stress an adult experiences on an auto trip is ten times worse for young kids. Boredom, claustrophobia, fidgety car crankiness: kids are subject to all of these, and they don't have all those wonderful grown-up worries to keep them alert and happy and distracted.

After the child has eaten junk food, fought with his sister, taken a nap, played electronic hand-held games, and fought with his sister, then what?

There are, in fact, several worry-based games that adults can play with children to pass the time and keep the youngsters—and their parents—amused.

"Who Can Tell Me What 'Toxic' Means?"

Try these Worry Games for Little Kids on Long Car Trips

1. *HAZMAT:* Select an arbitrary time period for the game, e.g., twenty minutes. Start the clock when the first person points out an abbreviation for a dangerous substance or something equally worrisome on a sign or a truck, for one point. The first person who correctly states what the abbreviation stands for also wins one point. Examples: "HAZMAT," for "hazardous material"; "NONPOT" for "nonpotable"; "TOXWAS," for "toxic waste"; "HOMA SCRA," for "home-made scrapple." When time is up, the person with the most points wins.

2. *Flammable:* Children scan the highway in search of trucks whose cargo could be dangerous. One point goes to the child who spies one, but only if he or she can explain why the contents could be something to worry about. If not, the kid loses one point, and another player gets the chance to worry about the cargo. Flammable liquids (e.g., gasoline, liquid oxygen) are obvious; dangerous cargo might allow for more creativity: cattle that could spread mad cow disease, rocking chairs that could spill all over the road, and so on. Adults will need to exercise some discretion to determine the validity of the danger, but remember, the purpose is to promote worry, pass the time— and have fun! The first player to reach a designated number of points wins.

3. *Cheese it!:* Children spend the entire trip on the lookout for traffic cops. First child to spot one gets one point. If the driver feels that the cop would have pulled the car over had the cop not been spotted, the kid gets an extra point. Keep playing until you reach your destination. The child with the most points wins.

The Secret Pleasures of Auto-Neuroticism

Americans might have "a love affair with the automobile," as some claim, but the most intense feelings arise when something goes wrong with their car.

From Oy To Joy

Worry	Benefit
I have a feeling I'm getting lousy mileage.	Repeated trips to gas station can translate into frequent-flier miles on credit card, leading to free trip to fabulous Aruba!
I think my car is creating more pollution than it really should.	Your help in spreading poisons will force the government to enact tougher auto emissions standards, ensuring better air for all.
Something's going to go any day now on this heap.	When it does, you'll be forced to get a new car—with a cool new audio system and more cup holders.
I feel guilty wanting to buy an SUV.	Guilt is sign of sensitivity, and the first step toward solving the problem. Your next car will be electric, once they make them bigger and faster.
I can't believe I let the guy talk me into the rally package, the sterling silver wheels, the GPS system, and the extended warranty.	You're helping stimulate the economy, advancing technology, and showing a fine aesthetic sensibility. You're a hero.

TRAVEL

Worry Your Way Around the World

One of the best things about worrying is that we can easily take our worries with us wherever we go. They accompany us on every journey, from the quickie weekend mountain getaway to the major overseas business trip. Even if circumstances require that we, say, change our identity and live under an assumed name in a different state, we retain our ability to worry.

And travel itself offers a vast, rich repertoire of things to worry about. Worrying about a journey of a thousand miles begins now, with worrying about a single step.

Let's Go! Not

If you're worried about whether to take a vacation—the cost, the time away, the fear of the unknown, the risk of getting sick—give in. Don't go! Immediately, the many benefits of not traveling begin to accrue. Naturally, they vary according to the destination not traveled to.

The Road Not Taken

Destination	Benefits of Not Going
Rome, Italy	No need to learn Italian; can eat spaghetti more cheaply in local restaurants.
Buffalo, New York	Avoid cold winters and insufferable summer honeymooners at Niagara Falls.
Ulan Bator, Mongolia	Avoid eating yaks.
Canberra, Australia	Avoid confusion of crossing equator; don't have to explain to everyone why you decided to go there.
Beijing, China	Avoid disorientation from not being able to read or sound out writing on signs, menus, or newspapers; tired of Chinese food anyway.
Nice, France	Save money; can hold on to fantasy of someday visiting and falling in love with the south of France and moving there.

If You Do Go, Be Open to New Worries

To travel to a foreign country, either for business or pleasure, is to leave behind every familiar component of your life and willingly surround yourself with strangeness. Nothing can be taken for granted. Everything becomes a fit subject for worry.

Thus, what happens to the worrier when he arrives in a foreign country is roughly what happened to Superman when he arrived on Earth from Krypton. His powers (of worrying) become superhuman. He is able to think about, and worry about, things that no normal stay-at-home human can even think about worrying about!

The results can be magnificent. When we worry about a problem, we often take steps to prevent it, forestall it, or solve it. We achieve an expansion in our minds, our sensibilities, our very souls. If, as the old cliché put it, travel is broadening, then worried travel is *really* broadening.

Language

The biggest and most ubiquitous issue encountered by international travelers is language. The normal exigencies of daily life are rendered much more difficult when you cannot understand, or be understood by, the people around you.

At home, for example, if you get food poisoning, you call a doctor or an ambulance, or take yourself to an emergency room. You worry about the diagnosis, the lingering effects of the disease, the expense of your treatment, and what will be required for your recovery.

But what do you do on, say, Leros Island? How do you say "food poisoning" in Greek? How do you call an ambulance? *What* do you call an ambulance? What are the names of the drugs? Will you be able to understand the doctor's explanation of the problem and what needs to be done?

Even mundane travel concerns—getting lost, needing a rest room, ordering from a menu, yelling at a pickpocket—become vexing challenges if you don't speak the language.

This is where worrying can pay off big time.

In learning the language of a foreign destination, the unworried traveler, naively unmindful of all the bad things that can happen, studies a few simple tourist phrases: "Excuse me," "Thank you," "The check, please," and "That's too expensive." But the dedicated worrier, obsessed with possible difficulties both profound and trivial, makes it his business to learn much more of the tongue in question. And what could be more enjoyable than conversing with people you meet abroad, in their own language?

The contrast between the phrases learned by the unworried and the worried travelers could not be more stark. Below are examples of what each typically arrives in a foreign country prepared to say. They are arranged by sightseeing location.

IN A MUSEUM

Unworried traveler: *Where is the rest room?*

Worried traveler: *The museum is on fire. The ventilation system is faulty. Where is my wife? I demand a refund. These muffins are stale. This poster is wrinkled. I can't hear the guide. The gift shop is not supposed to be closed yet.*

IN A CATHEDRAL

Unworried traveler: *Is that painting by Raphael?*

Worried traveler: *This bell tower is very high—is it safe to climb these steps? Are those people over there lepers? Why is it so cold? Is that nun glaring at me because I'm wearing shorts? Aren't those candles a fire hazard? Is there a rest room at the top of the tower?*

AT A FOUNTAIN ON A PLAZA

Unworried traveler: *This is very beautiful and refreshing.*

Worried traveler: *Is this water clean? Will I get sick if it splashes on me? Does the money people throw in there go to some church, or to terrorists? Why aren't those children being supervised? Shouldn't they be in school? I think my camera has been stolen and I am catching a cold.*

Schools of Worry

The ordinary person confronts the many things that can go wrong while traveling abroad, throws up her hands, and hopes for the best. But the dedicated worrier embraces these potential disasters and acts to anticipate them. She turns a modest five-day excursion to London,

Rio, or Singapore into nothing less than a liberal arts semester abroad, worthy of academic credit in a wide range of subjects.

College of Anxiety-Based Knowledge

Fretting about a trip inspires advanced learning.

Worry	Response	Subjects
Dealing with foreign currency; being cheated in commercial transactions	Learn the conversion equation to change local currency to and from dollars	Subjects Mastered: Mathematics, international finance
Contracting local diseases for which traveler has no immunity	Study local sanitation habits, sources of food and water, health-care system	Subjects Mastered: Immunology, ecology, biology, pharmacology
Being mugged, robbed, or kidnapped	Learn about government, neighborhoods, drug trade, political unrest	Subjects Mastered: History, political science, sociology, criminology
Getting lost	Practice using compass and GPS device, reading maps, asking for directions	Subjects Mastered: Geography, cartography, foreign languages

Exploration: Looking for Trouble

There are other kinds of travel besides the kind that involves seeking out foreign cultures, peoples, and civilizations. To many, travel means the deliberate *avoidance* of civilization, in favor of exploring forests, lakes, mountains, rivers, oceans, and deserts.

This mode of travel, which we will call "exploration," would seem to involve the radical rejection of worrying. If visiting Bogota is rife with worry, surely wandering across the Sahara or climbing K2 is its complete opposite.

And yet no one would suggest that there is nothing to worry about while trekking across a vast desert or climbing a dangerous, ice-covered mountain. True, there are fewer subjects for worry on the southwestern face of Everest than in the West End of London. But with the reduction in the quantity of worries comes a corresponding increase in their quality.

This is the secret to the allure of exploration—and "extreme" sports such as skydiving and bungee jumping. In all these activities, the cluttered bag of assorted worries one lugs around Sydney or Moscow is exchanged for a single small, portable, devastatingly essential worry: Will I die?

For the accomplished worrier, it is the extreme worry about the answer to that question that makes the activity so exhilarating and desirable. The greater the perceived risk, the greater the worry, the greater the joy.

Joy vs. Danger

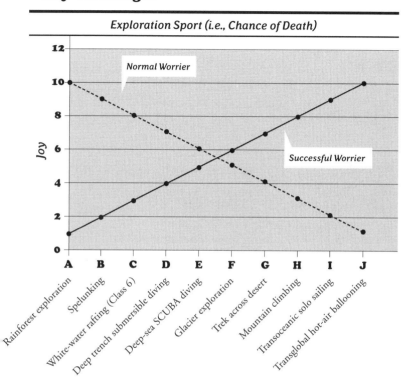

Exploration Sport (i.e., Chance of Death)

Normal Worrier

Joy

Successful Worrier

A — Rainforest exploration
B — Spelunking
C — White-water rafting (Class 6)
D — Deep trench submersible diving
E — Deep-sea SCUBA diving
F — Glacier exploration
G — Trek across desert
H — Mountain climbing
I — Transoceanic solo sailing
J — Transglobal hot-air ballooning

OMMMmmmigod, why did I volunteer
to be on the co-op board? What is my problem?
OMMMmman, am I a jackass... OMMMMmmmy
dental appointment is in three teeny-tiny weeks...
OMMMMMMMmmaybe I should cancel it...
OMMMMMmmerde!!!! I forgot to call my mother
back... I am the world's worst daughter...
OMMMMMMM Mmmy daughter...
now that's a case study in itself...
OMMmmy thighs look more gigantic
than ever in this leotard....
OOmmmm mmmm...

13

SELF-REALIZATION

Worry Your Way Awake and Aware

Health, wealth, sex, love, travel, interior decorating—they're all well and good for the physical world, but what if you're *deeper* than all that? What if you're the kind of person who pursues an inner quest for self-realization? Can worrying help?

Those people involved in Buddhism, yoga, meditation, psychotherapy, and other modes of self-inquiry might think of worrying as part of the problem. Worry is emblematic of "an attachment." It's "a loop." It's an expression of "neurotic fear." Such people might imagine that anxiety, because it focuses on something that doesn't exist, is irrational and an illusion. To them, worry is something to become aware of and expunge.

But don't be misled by the mindful. Even a dedicated self-realizer can reap huge benefits from worrying, by realizing that when we worry, one part of us (our inner, subconscious self) reveals to another part of us (our conscious self) something it's afraid of. Awareness of worry, then, is but the beginning of the discovery of the reality within. The more you worry, and the more you know you're worrying, the deeper your awareness and understanding of yourself.

Your goal is not to rid yourself of worry, because this would constitute a double denial—both of your true self, and of the nature of worry. Rather, your goal is to embrace and explore your worry, and hence to follow the path to enlightenment. The more we worry and *pay attention to it*, the more self-realized we become.

Recognizing Realization

If you've tried a variety of self-realization regimes and none of them feels right because you find you're still worried all the time, congratulate yourself! This worry might be a sign that, in the self-realization sweepstakes, you have already won!

If every available self-realization technique puts you off, if you find something to worry about in every one and are unable to get past these worries, perhaps the reason is that *you are already self-realized.*

Worrying Your Way Down the Path to Enlightenment

Once you commit to a strategy and begin your quest for self-realization, you will experience not only the worries you had when you began but also an entirely new array of worries about your chosen technique and your ability to succeed at it.

This is cause for celebration. Having worries about, say, yoga, when you have never had any before, is proof that yoga is changing you.

The more worries you experience, the more you can feel reassured that the technique is having the desired effect. The worries are a signal that you care, that you're involved with the technique and vulnerable to its ability to change your life.

Self-Realization Techniques and the Worries They Inspire

Technique: Traditional religion
Benefit: Not esoteric; familiar, socially accepted
Worry: Too old-fashioned to be credible

Technique: Mysticism—Sufism, Cabala, etc.
Benefit: Old as Methuselah; celebrities do it
Worry: Too esoteric and weird

Technique: New Age spiritual/science synthesis
Benefit: Modern, up-to-date
Worry: Too contrived to be effective

Technique: Scientology
Benefit: Very simple and efficient; all-encompassing
Worry: Founded too recently; cultish

Technique: Psychology-based therapy
Benefit: Effective
Worry: Too time-consuming and expensive

Technique: Yoga
Benefit: Not painful; health enhancing
Worry: Too slow and inefficient; may require lifestyle changes

Technique: Paranormal consultations—channeling, past lives, astrology, etc.
Benefit: Fast, cheap
Worry: Too far-out and specious

Technique: Zen Buddhism, meditation, and "sitting"
Benefit: Serious and respectable; psychologically credible
Worry: Proper sitting too painful; boring

Starting anywhere on the wheel, consider the self-realization technique named and the possible worried objection to it. Proceed to the next, in a clockwise direction, noting that each subsequent entry solves the problem of the previous one. If you go around the entire wheel and end up where you began without settling on any technique, congratulations. You're already self-realized.

A Study in Contrasts

Worrying and meditation at first would seem to be entirely different from each other, but in fact they have certain things in common. Worry is to meditation as a Palm Pilot is to a desktop computer. You can do more with the desktop, but to do so you have to stay at the desk, with those papers and yesterday's coffee mug and the curled-up Post-Its all around. But you can take the Palm Pilot to a party!

Top Five Ways Worrying and Meditation Are Alike

1. Both take place in the privacy of your own head.
2. Both feel like mental events that happen to you, not thoughts you can control.
3. Neither requires special equipment, money, or good weather.
4. Both can be done while just sitting around.
5. Neither makes noise, usually.

Top Five Ways in Which Meditation and Worrying Are Different

1. Meditation makes you nervous; worrying makes you afraid.
2. Meditation causes some people to laugh at you; worrying causes some people to avoid you.
3. Meditation gives you a headache; worrying causes you to lose your hair.
4. Meditation must be learned; worrying comes naturally.
5. Those who can, worry; those who can't, meditate.

Am I There Yet?

Common Worries Concerning Self-Realization	Joyous Consequence of Worries
I'll never get there. I'm too trapped in my personality/ego/games/neuroses, etc.	If I can say that, then it's working! I'm getting there!
There *is* no "there." I'm kidding myself. This is all an exercise in narcissistic self-involvement.	If I can say that, then it's working! I'm getting there!
I will get there, but I'll have to change my life. I'll feel resentful about all the changes I'll have to make.	If I can say that, then it's working! I'm getting there!
I'll get there, but I'll fall back into old, bad habits and patterns.	If I can say that, then it's working! I'm getting there!
My therapist/sensei/guru is a charlatan.	If I can say that, then it's working! I'm getting there!
The more I progress, the more I'll be alienated from my friends/spouse.	If I can say that, then it's working! I'm getting there!
The more I progress, the less my friends/spouse will be able to see that I'm right. They won't understand.	If I can say that, then it's working! I'm getting there!
This is costing a fortune.	If I can say that, then it's working! I'm getting there!
I'll get there, but it won't be wonderful or transforming enough. It'll be disappointing.	If I can say that, then it's working! I'm getting there!
I'll get there, but in order to stay there I'll have to become a weirdo.	If I can say that, then it's working! I'm getting there!

The Flow of Worry

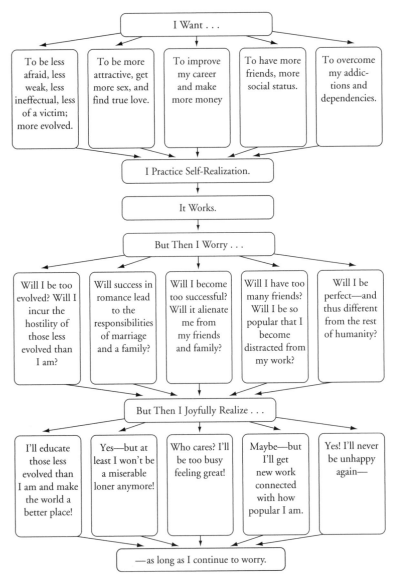

I Want . . .

| To be less afraid, less weak, less ineffectual, less of a victim; more evolved. | To be more attractive, get more sex, and find true love. | To improve my career and make more money | To have more friends, more social status. | To overcome my addictions and dependencies. |

I Practice Self-Realization.

It Works.

But Then I Worry . . .

| Will I be too evolved? Will I incur the hostility of those less evolved than I am? | Will success in romance lead to the responsibilities of marriage and a family? | Will I become too successful? Will it alienate me from my friends and family? | Will I have too many friends? Will I be so popular that I become distracted from my work? | Will I be perfect—and thus different from the rest of humanity? |

But Then I Joyfully Realize . . .

| I'll educate those less evolved than I am and make the world a better place! | Yes—but at least I won't be a miserable loner anymore! | Who cares? I'll be too busy feeling great! | Maybe—but I'll get new work connected with how popular I am. | Yes! I'll never be unhappy again— |

—as long as I continue to worry.

The Zen of Meditation and Worry

Meditate about your worrying. Worry about your meditating.

Nothing Succeeds Like (Worrying About) Success

Worrying about not succeeding at self-realization is perfectly understandable—and, as we have seen, perfectly wonderful! But what if, by some miracle, you actually do succeed at your quest? Does that mean there's nothing left to worry about?

Of course not. Success never means there is nothing more to worry about. It means there are new things to worry about, and success-related things can be just as worrisome as the things you worried about before attaining self-realization.

The latent worry in success is referred to in the proverb "Be careful what you wish for—you may get it." But this is an incomplete expression of the concept, and an unnecessarily negative way of expressing what is actually a hopeful, even thrilling observation about the things we wish for, and what happens when those wishes come true. A more complete statement might be the following: "Be careful what you wish for. Then, when you get it, have a ball worrying, both about what you've gotten, and about the other things you might wish for and get and worry about."

Anyone can worry about not succeeding (and they should), and a moderately practiced worrier can worry about wishing for the wrong thing. You'll know you've become a skilled worrier when you begin worrying about the consequences of success.

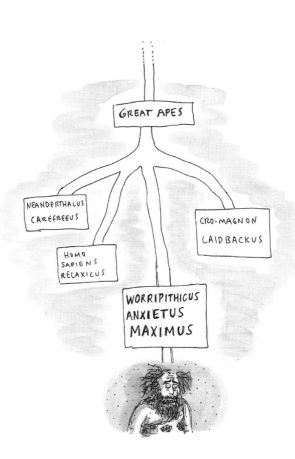